TO WIN THESE RIGHTS

TO WIN
THESE RIGHTS

A Personal Story of the CIO in the South

by Lucy Randolph Mason

FOREWORD BY ELEANOR ROOSEVELT

INTRODUCTION BY GEORGE SINCLAIR MITCHELL

HARPER & BROTHERS   PUBLISHERS   NEW YORK

*To the men and women who
through the union movement
are creating a better South.*

CONTENTS

FOREWORD

by ELEANOR ROOSEVELT

THIS BOOK by Lucy Randolph Mason, entitled *To Win These Rights*, is really the story of Miss Mason's work for the CIO in the South. This mild looking, soft spoken gentlewoman inherited from her forebears in Virginia a fiery fighting spirit and a passion for justice and truth valuable to the CIO and to its difficulties during the first days of organizing in the South.

This is a personal story of the CIO in the South and pen sketches of the men who took part in this experiment.

I am proud to have known Miss Mason. I have admired her work and her courage. I hope there are other members in her family to follow in her footsteps to see that American democracy which is based on equality of opportunity and justice for all is the best that can be achieved.

This book is a bit of history, a part of history that we will be proud of in the future, and I think the South will be proud that one of its own people wrote this record of a really remarkable piece of work for the achievement of democracy.

INTRODUCTION

THE BEST of all the stories about Lucy Mason is one she won't tell in the book. A Virginia town, far up the James River, has a newish factory. Something to do with textiles. Twice the union had tried to organize it and worked up a Labor Board election. Each time, at the crucial moment, the Lions Club had "scandalized" the union, and the vote went the wrong way. For the third effort the union sent Miss Lucy in ahead of time. Her business was to tame the Lions.

Lucy talked to this one and that and finally found herself in the office of a doctor, who by all accounts was the King. If he could be convinced, things would go better. So here was Miss Lucy, arguing the civil rights of the workers, when into the doctor's office lounged a tall fellow, a bit roughly dressed, with leggings. He wasn't introduced, and Lucy could only guess that he was a prosperous cattle-farmer. He just listened, but when Lucy was through he said:

"Lady, I would like to ask you some questions. What's back of you? Who sent you here, and what salary do you make? And by what right do you come into the State of Virginia talking all this about civil rights?"

"Young man! You've asked for it, and I'll tell you!"

Whereupon she called the roll of the famous Virginians, many of them statesmen in the cause of plain men's rights, to whom she was kin.

George Mason was her great-great-great-grandfather. He wrote the Virginia Declaration of Rights, which became the Bill of Rights in the Constitution of the United States; he drew the first Constitution of Virginia, model for that of many other States; and his thought is deep into the legal foundations of American life.

Three of her kinsmen signed the Declaration of Independence.

Chief Justice John Marshall was her mother's great-great-uncle.

For good measure, in the lush Colonial days, all the galaxy of notables clustered in the line of William Randolph of Turkey Island —the Carters, the Beverleys, the Bollings, the Chichesters; a genealogist's dream!

If the be-legginged gentleman questioned her Confederate titles, her great-grandfather, James Murray Mason, shared honors with Slidell as the Confederacy's envoy to Britain.

General Lee was her father's near cousin, and her father himself saw gallant service in Mosby's and other famous Confederate brigades.

And in the wars of this century, brothers had served and one had died for America's cause.

"Madam," said our friend, "I don't know what the C.I.O. pays you, but I am sure you are worth it."

There is an instructive comparison between George Mason in his time and Lucy Mason in hers. Helen Hill's life of Mason gives a clue.

After the ties with Britain had been cut, Mason played a leading role in hammering out at Williamsburg the new and independent civil community. There on the hat pegs of the Raleigh Tavern he would find both the plumed felts of the Tidewater gentry and the rough caps of the back-country farmers. Mason's task was to shape a state which could guarantee the rights of both groups. He achieved it, and in so doing set the basis for the identical achievement in the Constitution of the United States. His instrument was the Bill of Rights, which in law gave to every freeman the liberties of the richest citizen.

Fur caps and plumes have left our hat racks, but in an industrial society divisions are deep. And Lucy Randolph Mason has put all her life into getting for the disadvantaged of today the stature and strength that every American knows is his right.

Between those great builders of our independence and Lucy's time, the South turned to a less promising way of thought. And because of that, Lucy's own father, as a clergyman on pittance stipends at Drake's Branch and Marietta, knew a suffering region. But the clergyman's daughter, having in her bones the hurts of the South, remembered the human hope of old George and his friends, and set about recapturing that full vision for the people of the South.

This is the book that tells how she worked.

GEORGE SINCLAIR MITCHELL

PREFACE

THIS IS my story about the CIO in the South these past fifteen years. It is partly an account of my own small share in the movement, and partly what I could draw directly from many persons with whom I have worked. It is honest reporting, from them and from me.

The South still has heavy concern with the ideas of an earlier period; it faces too slowly the new times and new needs. Yet in our shadowed democracy there grows among the people a brave determination to produce human equality and justice.

It has been my good fortune to be associated closely with that welling-up of promise in the South, wherein men and women have sought a tool with which to win their hopes.

My years with the industrial unions of the CIO have taught me that out of them come the true aristocrats of our times: leaders who earnestly seek to serve their fellow men.

Few are the books, however small, which make their way into print without help from many people. My own indebtedness reaches to scores of friends, and my gratitude to them travels about with me. Some have been so very generous of time and helpfulness that their names should be written out. Among them are Josephine Wilkins, Rebecca Gershon, George Sinclair Mitchell, Mrs. Charles W. Skinner, Richard Conn (who first suggested the whole idea), David S. Burgess and John G. Ramsay, who read the manuscript bit by bit. Director John V. Riffe and all his staff gave me encouragement and every cooperation. Hours of patient work were done by Ethel Stanley, Mrs. R. W. Thrasher, Beth Nicholson and Katherine Norton.

LUCY RANDOLPH MASON

Atlanta, Georgia
July 1, 1952

TO WIN THESE RIGHTS

Chapter I

BACKGROUND FOR ACTION

CLARENS, where I was born on July 26, 1882, is a long, two-story white house on the Episcopal Seminary Hill, near Alexandria, Virginia. It was then the home of my great-aunt Miss Virginia Mason and her sister Ida.

At that time our family was living in Shepherdstown, West Virginia, where my father, Reverend Landon Randolph Mason, was the Episcopal minister. Mother was Lucy Ambler before her marriage, and her father was Reverend John Cary Ambler, an Episcopal missionary to the mountains of West Virginia, whose visits when we were young were occasions of great joy to all of us. When I was six weeks old, Mother returned to Shepherdstown with the new baby.

Father's first parish had been at Drakes Branch, in the southern part of Virginia. He had two or three country "missions" as part of his Drakes Branch Parish. Mother used to say that the salary was $500 a year, paid mostly in black-eyed peas and bacon.

Sometimes in my CIO work I have heard it said that I could not appreciate the needs of working people because I "was born with a silver spoon in my mouth." To dispel any illusions as to the financial status of the family, here are other bits in our history. In Shepherdstown, father's second parish, the salary was $900. We moved to Marietta, Georgia, when I was eight years old. The salary there was $1500. We stayed less than a year because father thought the available schools unsatisfactory for the education of the chil-

1

dren. He accepted a call to Richmond with a top salary there of $2600. A modest rectory was supplied in all of these places.

My mother had to be a remarkable financier to make the money cover the needs of the family and help the boys attend the University of Virginia. My brothers used to get jobs in summer vacations, by which they contributed to the cost of going to college.

When I was twenty-two I rented a typewriter, bought a shorthand book, taught myself stenography and typing, and became a contributor to the family funds. My first job paid the magnificent sum of $5 a week, with a work-day from 8:30 A.M. to 6 P.M. I soon got a better one and moved up in compensation. In less than two years I was earning $75 a month, a large salary for a stenographer in those days.

"UNTO THE LEAST OF THESE"

Both mother and father had a strong sense of social responsibility. It was part of their religious conviction. Their deep concern for human welfare led them into many unusual contacts. Father would respond to calls for help from poverty stricken families who had no connection with our congregation. I remember his carrying a bushel of coal on his back, from a store to the home of a destitute family, one winter day when an eighteen inch snow had stopped all traffic. That was typical of his way of answering calls for help. In times of epidemics such as scarlet fever, he went wherever he was needed, often sitting up all night with some ill or dying person.

One night a group of men were together at the Commonwealth Club in Richmond, talking about father and his life of self-denial and service. One of the men said,

"Mr. Mason is the most beloved man in Richmond—it is time somebody was doing something for him."

Another man said, "Let's give him a trip to England this summer."

A quick canvass was made and the men in the club that evening raised $500, enough for a modest trip abroad in those distant years, and appointed a committee to take it to father.

Being a frugal young woman I had saved enough to take some one to England with father. I wanted mother to go, but she had many reasons for not undertaking such a trip and insisted that I should go. So I had my first trip to England at the age of twenty-six and never regretted spending my savings that way.

Mother had a Bible class Sunday afternoons in the State Penitentiary, located in Richmond. Many of the men she met there came to our house when they were released. Some of them stayed with us while looking for work. They used the third-floor bedroom next to mine, but none of us ever had any fear of their doing harm. Through these contacts, mother discovered the atrocious cruelties that were perpetrated within the prison walls. She and her friend Mrs. Whitehead, and Dr. Carrington, a private medical practitioner who gave part of his time to serving the penitentiary inmates on a salary basis, decided to tell what they knew of the barbarities in that institution. Another friend of mother's, Mr. Charles Baughman, who was in the printing and stationery business, donated the cost of printing leaflets that were distributed throughout the state.

The public was shocked by these revelations. The penitentiary authorities proclaimed that owing to a smallpox scare in Norfolk, one hundred miles away, the prison must be closed to all visitors. They kept a quarantine on the penitentiary for a year or more. But the revelations made by mother led to some immediate reforms and doubtless contributed to the sweeping changes that took place some years after her death.

One morning Mother received through the mail a newspaper clipping about a young girl who had killed her baby and tried to kill herself. She had been committed to jail. Mother never knew who eased his conscience by mailing her that clipping, but she went immediately to the jail and was permitted to see the girl, who was in a desperate state of mind. We knew where Mother had gone and were not surprised when a phone call came from her at supper time saying she must spend the night in the cell with the girl, who still threatened to kill herself.

Mother and Father practiced what Jesus said when he described the final test that made men fit to inherit the Kingdom of God. They took in and fed the stranger; they refreshed the spirit of the thirsty; they gave clothes to those who lacked them; they visited the sick; and they went to those in prison. They knew they served God as they cared for His children, remembering the Command "Love thy neighbor as thyself." Indirectly, Mother served the lepers of the world, since she raised money for the Leper Mission that housed, fed, and clothed them. The Mission also helped promote the cures for leprosy that have brought many formerly afflicted people back to health. Somewhere in India there is a cottage in a leper colony which bears her name.

Social Service in Richmond

When I was fourteen, a missionary's sermon made me want to be a missionary myself. Later, I recognized that religion can be put to work right in one's own community. It was this belief that took me into the Equal Suffrage League, and later the League of Women Voters, both of which were interested in labor and social legislation. I served on the boards of a number of social service organizations, and was keenly interested in better understanding and cooperation between the white and Negro races.

While still young I was impressed by man's inhumanity to man, and eager to arouse the public conscience on the need for such legislation as required safety appliances on dangerous machinery; workmen's compensation for men injured on the job; shorter hours for women workers (Virginia's nominal ten-hour day law was a dead-letter statute and unenforceable), protection of children from too early or dangerous employment.

Eight of the ten years I worked as a stenographer were spent in the corporation law offices of Allen Caperton Braxton. Though office hours were long in those days, I still found time for volunteer work. When Mr. Braxton's death in 1914 dissolved that firm, several excellent stenographic and other business jobs were open to me; but when the Young Women's Christian Association offered me a place on its staff as industrial secretary, at less salary than the commercial offers, I joyfully accepted. I was with the Richmond "Y" from the fall of 1914 until April, 1918.

In January, 1918, a blow came to our family. Mother died of a coronary thrombosis. For her it was translation—for us sad hearts. She was a vital, beautiful woman, even at sixty-nine, with intelligence, wit, charm, and a boundless love for her fellow men.

Father had retired shortly before her death and was then seventy-six years old. He was handicapped by deafness and cataract. Someone had to be at home with him. My only sister, Ida, had married a banker and lived in Alexandria. Randolph Fitzhugh, the oldest of us, a teacher and artist, had volunteered at thirty-nine and was soon to be in France. (Randolph was killed in the summer of 1918 in the fighting north of Belleau Wood.) Landon, a younger brother, was in the British Army, and John Ambler was an industrial engineer and lived with his family in Baltimore. So I stopped work, John supplied the money, and for five and a half years all my spare time went into volunteer activities with various social agencies.

Although my friends Hermine and Carrie Moore lived with us and were good to Father, I limited my volunteer activities to Richmond and rarely spent a night away from home. During this period I was president first of the Richmond Equal Suffrage League and later of the League of Women Voters.

Cooperating with Labor Unions

When I first became "union conscious" I do not know. I suppose it grew out of my concern because of the industrial accidents that happened to so many of the working people I knew, the long work days in Richmond's factories, laundries, stores, and everywhere else. These ten- and eleven-hour days were not only bad for the people who worked them, but disrupted normal family life. They burned my conscience and during my long life I have spent a lot of time laboring to shorten hours of work for both men and women.

It early became apparent that the best paid workers were union members, and they had an eight-hour day, with half of Saturday off. So it seemed natural that my sympathies and hopes should turn toward the unions. I remember that when I was still a stenographer there was a street railway drivers' strike and I avoided riding on street cars for the duration of the strike. There was a lot of snow and sleet that winter, and traveling on foot was not easy.

Early in life I joined the Union Label League. The label was used on garments made in factories whose workers were union members. The label meant better working conditions and wages. I searched diligently for clothing with labels, but rarely found any in Richmond stores. At least we League members asked questions and showed our interest in union-made goods. Frequently, I spoke to union meetings on this and other subjects. (Years later, in New York, I became a member of the International Ladies Garment Workers Union Label Committee, whose purpose was to win public support for clothes bearing this label.)

During the governorship of Westmoreland Davis we had strong support from him and his splendid secretary, Col. LeRoy Hodges. Those two worked together in accomplishing many reforms. Virginia owed them a special debt of gratitude for bringing about the complete reformation of the State Penitentiary and making it a place in which human beings might live.

At that time, the only organized body of men who stood by our women's organizations in fighting for progressive and humane legislative measures were the Virginia and Richmond Federations of Labor. During World War I, Samuel Gompers, president of the American Federation of Labor, appointed me "Virginia Chairman of the Committee on Women in Industry, of the National Advisory Committee on Labor." Usually such a post went to a union member or representative. This was my first union appointment.

My father died in June 1923 at the age of eighty-two, after a few days illness from acute appendicitis. He had never recovered from the deaths of his beloved wife and oldest son. Confidently anticipating reunion with them, his going was a consummation.

PROFESSIONAL WORK AGAIN

My volunteer days were at an end and professional work was taken up again. One of the first offers came from the Richmond

Young Women's Christian Association to be general secretary, which I accepted. A few days after this, I received a letter from Mrs. Florence Kelley, general secretary of the National Consumers League, asking me to come on her staff as southern secretary. That was a great temptation, for I would have given all my time to promoting labor and social legislation. But I preferred to remain in Richmond at that time, and had already accepted the secretaryship of the YWCA.

Mrs. Kelley was indignant. She wrote me on September 5, 1923:

> I consider it a calamity of national dimensions that, at this moment, you are bending your best energies to the work of a local organization of *any* kind, instead of sharing the vast opportunity to modernize the Supreme Court and the U. S. Constitution!
>
> This—no less—confronts all thinking women as the work of the hour. All effort to improve industrial conditions under the present Constitution, interpreted by the present Court, is purely academic.
>
> I note, with some slight feeling of consolation for this lost year, the ray of hope you hold out that, after a year, some arrangement different from the present one might be possible for you. And I hasten to point out that I waited nine years for Miss Dewson, and on one occasion four years for Pauline Goldmark, and in the end both came into this office.
>
> So, I am girding on the armor of patience for a year, trusting that the situation will then be such that you will consent to become Secretary for the southern states, or to assume any title that may be more to your taste than this.
>
> Yours always hopefully,
FLORENCE KELLEY

(By a strange coincidence, it was just nine years later that I walked into the office of the National Consumers League in New York as Mrs. Kelley's successor.)

The Richmond YWCA was blessed with an excellent administrator, Emma Zanzinger, as its general secretary for several years before I took that post. There was a good board and staff and an enthusiastic president in Mrs. J. Scott Parrish. Brownie Lee Jones, industrial and education secretary for four years, was unusually effective in opening people's minds to progressive ideas and contributed a great deal to making the Richmond Association a social force in the community. (Miss Jones later served the southern labor movement as director of the Southern School for Workers, and is now on the staff of the American Labor Education Service.)

Some of us were able to convince the Board of the YWCA that it had a concern for long hours of work and low pay for industrial workers, so the Association was frequently represented at legislative committee hearings on such matters. This sometimes led to unexpected occurrences. I recall one occasion when an Amendment to the Constitution permitting Federal regulation of child labor was under consideration. Mr. J. Scott Parrish was president of the Richmond Chamber of Commerce. Mrs. Parrish was president of the Richmond YWCA. On a Wednesday afternoon the boards of these two organizations met at the same time, about two blocks apart. Next morning, the paper carried a conspicuous story to the effect that the Chamber of Commerce Board had passed a resolution condemning the Child Labor Amendment, and at the same hour the YWCA Board had adopted a resolution favoring the Amendment!

The YWCA cooperated effectively with many other organizations and spread its influence over a wide circle. The Council of Social Agencies instituted a survey of the Negro community in Richmond for which I served as chairman of the committee on the economic status of Negroes. The findings and report resulting from that survey led to the reorganization of the Richmond Urban League and were useful for years to come in many other ways.

In the early winter of 1931 a group of church women from six southern states invited me to spend two months traveling in the South trying to create public opinion for better child labor laws and shorter hours of work for women.

I accepted and had an illuminating time. I met governors, legislators, newspaper editors, ministers, college professors, labor representatives, social workers, civic leaders—and manufacturers. This was the only period in which industrialists, or some of them, were glad to see someone who advocated both state and federal legislation to curtail hours of work. For 1931 was at the bottom of the Great Depression, millions of men and women formed an enormous pool of unemployed who would work under any conditions and for any wages, however low. The South's leading industry—cotton textiles—was in a terribly depressed condition. Over-production and full warehouses had resulted in a glutted market and depressed prices. In a frantic endeavor to meet competition by continually lowering costs, textile manufacturers had lengthened hours of work, resorted to almost general night work, and cut wages until seven or eight dollars a week was common pay.

The Cotton Texitle Institute had been formed by manufacturers in 1928 in a futile effort to get voluntary agreement on reducing hours, particularly at night, with no night work for women and minors under eighteen. It was hoped that this would eventually mean getting rid of night work completely. Compliance with these suggestions at its peak had resulted in about 85 per cent of the industry's "going along," at least for a short time. But the pressure of competition had continued and more and more companies were ceasing to regard the Institute's agreement.

Some of the cotton textile manufacturers who worked most diligently for the gentleman's agreement saw that national legislation was the only means of getting a sure foundation for limitation of hours and the other features agreed to but not carried out. Among these was Donald Comer, president of the Avondale Mills in Alabama. Mr. Comer later told me he had asked Senator Hugo Black to introduce a bill for a general eight-hour day as the only hope of curtailing production. That became the Black Six-hour Day Bill, and although it failed to pass, it helped in the passage of a bill for an eight-hour day which came later. Mr. Comer was an open advocate of federal regulation of child labor. He also supported the minimum wage section of the Cotton Textile NRA code.

Many outstanding northern textile industrialists were for national legislation on wages and hours. Such was the attitude of Mr. Harry Fitzgerald, president of the Dan River Mills in Virginia, one of the most ardent supporters of the voluntary agreement to limit hours adopted by the Textile Institute in 1928. His daughter Harriet Fitzgerald recently wrote me that he was one of the first to advocate the

Textile Institute's program for reduction of hours and had great hope
in the gentleman's agreement. He was disappointed by its failure,
and thereafter talked of a national legislative program for both limitation of hours and a bottom to wages. He felt the industry would
be bankrupt unless this could be done. She added that her father had
favored a national child labor law early in his career. "My father
supported Al Smith in the 1928 campaign," her letter continued,
with Smith's record in regard to labor legislation in New York State
open before him. I think he would have seen Mr. Roosevelt's program as the answer—but he died a few months before Roosevelt
was nominated."

In memory I can still see the lights in the cotton mills at night, as
I went about the South trying to promote the idea of both national
and state legislation to help stabilize the industry and stop the exces-
sive exploitation of the men, women, and children working in it.
These lights meant twelve-hour shifts for many of the workers—
without regular lunch periods—snacks eaten as machines were
tended.

After two months' travel in the southern states, I returned to the
YWCA in Richmond and wrote a pamphlet entitled "Standards for
Workers in Southern Industry." It was printed by the National Consumers League. Being the first compilation of the kind this pamphlet was widely used. Two years later, when the Roosevelt program
was being worked out, Frances Perkins distributed the pamphlet at
the first National Labor Legislation Conference after her appointment as Secretary of Labor.

The Cotton Textile Institute in 1932 asked the Consumers League
for five hundred copies which the Institute wished to distribute
among southern cotton manufacturers. At that time the Institute was
still putting its energies behind the voluntary agreement and wished
to use my pamphlet as leverage for the agreement—sort of "the big,
bad wolf of legislation will get you, unless you adopt voluntary
control of hours of work."

During the depths of the depression, the Richmond YWCA made
repeated efforts to attract public attention, through the newspapers

and otherwise, to the unemployment and consequent poverty so widely prevalent. But Richmond and Virginia were going through a period of Polly-Annaish confidence that a change for the better was just around the corner. We did, however, succeed in arousing the social workers over federal legislation for aid to the unemployed, and bringing pressure to bear on members of Congress.

Richmond was kind to me. No one knew in January, 1932, that I would be leaving in six months. So it was not a farewell when, at the YWCA annual meeting in January, a book of letters of appreciation was presented to me. I was almost overwhelmed, but managed to accept, graciously, I hope.

Six months later, just before I left Richmond, "a service of appreciation" was held in one of the leading Negro Baptist churches, whose pastor was my friend Dr. Gordon B. Hancock. That was one of the most moving occasions of my life. The church was packed. Organizations among the Negro community sponsored the service. I sat in the center of the chancel on what looked like a bishop's chair, with a towering back. The participants sat in a half circle facing the audience. When all the speeches had been made (all from memory), I was given the bound book of messages.

As I found myself the object of most warm appreciation, being credited with far more than I had ever accomplished, it suddenly occurred to me I would be called upon to reply. That almost spoiled the occasion until I saw a way of deliverance. When I began to speak I said that I did not know the person they had been describing —no one knew her, because she did not exist. But I was inspired by the picture they had painted out of the height of their imaginations, the breadth of their feeling, and the kindness of their hearts. So I transferred the burden of the praise to those who had spoken.

NATIONAL CONSUMERS LEAGUE

In the spring of 1932 I had a letter from Mary W. Dewson, chairman of the executive committee of the National Consumer's League, asking if I would consider a call to fill the office of general secretary. Mrs. Florence Kelley, who had been the first and only secretary of the League, had died and a successor was being sought. I accepted with humble joy, feeling too small for the work, but impelled to go into it. I had known Mrs. Kelley for years and greatly admired her. Mary Dewson (affectionately known as Molly) was a well-liked acquaintance whom I had met at various national conferences.

The League has had an honorable history. It was founded by churchmen of Christian and Jewish faiths, and by social workers and other public-spirited men and women. It was a newly formed organization when Florence Kelley went from Chicago to New York in 1899 as its secretary. Its purpose was to expose and fight sweatshop conditions in industry through "investigation, education and legislation."

Mrs. Kelley in 1909 attended an international conference on minimum-wage laws held in England, where such legislation was in effect. Ever after that she worked with unremitting vigor for minimum-wage laws in this country. When I was with the League I often called it the "consumers' conscience," for that is what Florence Kelley actually accomplished—she made people aware of the evil conditions under which goods were made, sold, and distributed, and made them feel responsible for doing something about them.

Mrs. Kelley was the daughter of a steel manufacturer who was thirty years in the U. S. House of Representatives. She used to recall that her father had given her an injunction she must live up to: "My generation has created industry," he would say, "your generation must humanize it." She spent her consecrated life doing just that.

One of Mrs. Kelley's most stalwart co-workers was Mary W. Dewson, a great woman who accomplished notable things and yet rarely got into the limelight. From the time I met Molly at a National League of Women Voters conference in Baltimore, soon after woman suffrage was gained, we had a bond in common—labor legislation for the amelioration of working conditions, and women's responsibility as citizens to bring this about.

After I had gone with the Consumers League, Molly told me that Mrs. Kelley had suggested me as her successor not long before she died. Two of her reasons were that my background would help me work effectively in the South, where working conditions were poor and labor laws few and weak; and that I was consecrated to improving the lot of working women.

Miss Dewson deserves a volume about her service to the best elements in the Democratic Party. She is a woman of honesty and great ability. The issues before the country were always the paramount fact with her—not the personalities of the candidates. After her work in directing the women's division in a considerable area during the 1928 presidential campaign, she was made chairman of the Democratic National Women's Division in the first Roosevelt campaign and did a notable job. Mrs. Roosevelt and Molly were friends of long standing and worked closely together in that campaign. I am indebted to Mary Dewson for introducing me to Mrs. Roosevelt, who I think is the world's greatest woman, and one of its few greatest citizens. She was one of the Consumers League's vice presidents and partly because of that I was to see her fairly often in the future. A gain for women made by Miss Dewson was the fifty-fifty participation by women on all Democratic Party committees. After some years of working on this, she saw that her urgings had prevailed and the matter was, in her words, "cinched in the nominating Convention of 1940." Molly Dewson was the first woman to be vice-chairman of the Democratic National Committee.

When I went to live in New York in September, 1932, the Great Depression was at its worst. The New York papers told what was happening. Stories of unemployment, short working weeks, starvation wages, and human want and misery were prevalent. For instance, in a downtown industrial district in New York a garment manufacturer advertised for skilled workers at ten dollars a week. The police had to break up the riot as a thousand women struggled to be up front and have a chance at a job.

In Cleveland, Ohio, a merchant advertised for ten experienced salesladies at eight dollars a week. The mob that formed outside his store was so great that the pressure of women against one another resulted in the smashing of a plate-glass window. Some women had to be taken to the hospital.

The sweatshop type of garment manufacturer got wages down to five or six dollars a week, with no pay for beginners. In the garment plants, textile mills, and tobacco factories of the South, wages were unbelievably low and completely inadequate to support workers and their families.

We decided that the National Consumers League should publicize conditions in every way possible. We called a conference on labor standards, sent out questionnaires in all directions and asked social agencies to give us all the facts they could. Information poured in. Mrs. Emily Sims Marconnier, the able associate secretary of the League, found free-lance writers who got material from our office and made it the basis for magazine stories. Labor unions helped us gather facts and publicize them.

During the formative period of the NRA Codes in the summer of 1933, I spent a good deal of time in Washington and frequently spoke before code commissioners for the consumers' interest in good labor conditions and wages. In industries with a considerable amount of union organization, the unions took care of getting witnesses before the commissioners. I appeared chiefly in those unorganized industries whose workers had no means of making effective presentations—they were called the "sweated industries," denoting low wages and often poor working conditions, but mainly overwork and underpay.

The first code to be heard was that of the Textile Industry. For finally that industry was seeking national wage and hour control. I spoke on the need of such controls and for higher standards than the manufacturers had asked. When I had finished my twenty-minute talk, the commissioner in a courteous way, asked if I would answer some questions—which I was delighted to do. He asked me what the textile people would do with their money if wages were raised. I said they would spend it; they would get more and better food; shoes for the children so they could go to school in cold weather; the women in the family—and men and boys too—would get some better clothes to wear to church and on the street. They might go to a movie once in a while; and even buy an old car and some gasoline to go to see their people. In fact, I said, the workers would do with their higher pay exactly what President Roosevelt hoped they would—spend it and put the money into circulation. This was greeted by roars of laughter and much hand-clapping. The northern textile manufacturers beamed upon me, most of the southerners scowled.

I remember particularly the code hearing on crushed stone, sand, and gravel, obviously a low-wage industry according to the testimony. It was claimed that the majority of the workers in this industry in the South were Negroes, ignorant and unskilled, who, if they made more money, would work only two or three days a week and then get drunk and throw away their money.

One of the southern employers said that if these colored workers should get wages of 25¢ an hour it would *demoralize the economic and social status of the whole South*! Again, I made a statement for higher wages, and answered a number of questions. Some of the younger southerners came up after the hearing and said they entirely approved what I had said, for competition in low labor standards was not only bad for individual workers but for their industry and for the whole southern economy.

At the NRA code hearings in Washington I met many outstanding union men and women. Also in New York my work took me to meetings which were attended by labor's representatives. Prominent among them were Sidney Hillman, president of the Amalgamated Clothing Workers, and Jacob S. Potofsky, then the union's vice-president, now its president. Also David Dubinsky, president of the International Ladies Garment Workers Union, and many of his staff. These two great unions of men's and women's garment workers had so completely organized the older portions of their industries that strikes were things of the past. Labor-management peace was maintained by settling differences through mediation, conciliation, and arbitration—around the conference table, not on the picket line.

Meanwhile, Molly Dewson had forgotten how tired she was when the Roosevelt campaign of 1932 ended, and had gone to work reviving interest in Minimum Wage Legislation. Benjamin V. Cohen, one of the most brilliant of Roosevelt's legal staff and drafter of much New Deal legislation, put his mind on a model "fair wage" law for states that would not be thrown out by the Supreme Court. Seven states passed such laws in the following sessions, and the Supreme Court sustained them.

Tom Corcoran and Ben Cohen also prepared the Fair Labor Standards Act which Senator Black introduced and had passed in the Senate, but when difficulties arose in the House, Frances Perkins, Secretary of Labor, had her counsel work on a new and much shorter act. This bill passed the House and was the basis of the bill which became law. The Fair Labor Practices Act of June, 1938, was a result of much that had gone before. The Act set up a basic eight-hour day and forty-hour week, with a definite sum for a national minimum wage. It also provided for increasing the minimum wage for an industry through industry committees of employers, employees, and the public.

About the end of June, 1937, I had gone to Washington to speak before the Senate Committee on Labor in behalf of the Fair Labor Practices Bill. Mr. John L. Lewis appeared as a witness for the bill and was the first speaker. I had met him briefly once at a dinner meeting in honor of Frances Perkins, newly appointed Secretary of Labor. In connection with the purchase of his home in Alexandria, Mr. Lewis had met my brother-in-law, Taylor Burke, President of Burke and Herbert Bank. The banker and union leader liked each other and had become friends.

I admired Mr. Lewis' brilliant leadership of the industrial union movement and took the opportunity to speak to him while we were waiting for the hearing to begin. He was cordial and spoke highly of Taylor Burke. I was staying with the Burkes, and that evening, I expressed an often felt desire to go back South to live, where I could work with organized labor and interracial groups. I was particularly concerned with the status of Negroes in the new unions.

My sister laughed and said, "Why not try John Lewis?"

Her lightly spoken words rang a bell for me. "Ida, you are joking," I said, "but that may prove to be the smartest thing you ever said to me."

The result was that the next evening Taylor called Mr. Lewis and suggested a talk with him, to which Mr. Lewis responded by dropping by in less than an hour.

It was a delightful evening. Mr. Lewis is a remarkably well informed man and interesting conversationalist. He was impressed by the idea that I might work in the South as a publicist and public relations representative for the CIO and particularly in behalf of the Textile Workers Organizing Committee. He practically settled the matter then and there, but said that inasmuch as Sidney Hillman was director of the organizing drive in the Textile Industry, I must see him before the matter could be concluded. He said he would speak to Mr. Hillman, and after that I should see him.

When I returned to New York I found Mr. Hillman out of town, but talked on the telephone with Jack Potofsky, his right-hand man in the Amalgamated Clothing Workers, and asked if I might see him. As soon as Mr. Potofsky realized that I wanted to work in the field of public relations and publicity for the CIO in the South, he said: "Do you mean you will live and work in the South all the time?" When I said yes, he answered: "You don't need to see me about that. I heard you talk about unions when you spoke in St. Paul's Church in Richmond. I told you then that you ought to stay in the South all the time. I am all for this. I will tell Sidney we ought to put you down there and he will be for it too."

Soon after, Mr. Hillman and I did have a talk and he said that I would be working under him as southern director of organization for textiles and clothing, and under Mr. Lewis as president of the CIO. He said, "John is generous and I am stingy, so you'd better deal with him when it comes to salary."

Mr. Lewis spoke to me about my salary and I told him what my last two salaries had been with the YWCA and the National Consumers League—$3600 and $5000 respectively. I said I was willing to have a salary from the CIO of $3600. Mr. Lewis replied, "You will get $5000." I protested this was too much for working people to pay me. He replied that he was not willing to pay me less than I had been receiving with the League.

I went to work for the CIO in July, 1937, and three months later

I sent in my first salary and expense account with the salary at $300 a month—$3600 a year. In about 1945 when there was a general salary increase, I accepted $4000 a year.

The important concern to me was that my services might be worth something real to the industrial union movement. Every day of this new life was an adventure—every assignment in the field a challenge. Meeting and talking with the union folk was the inspiration, and coming back to the office to tell the story was the fun. My rewards were in the commendation my fellow workers gave me.

Chapter II

TO WORK WITH THE CIO

THE SOUTH IN 1937

UNTIL THE coming of the industrial unions of the CIO, beginning in 1935-36, the South had little union organization. Most of what union strength there was represented the craft unions of the American Federation of Labor. Successful unionism among workers in the mass production industries was limited to the United Mine Workers, which had practically done its organizing job by 1933. Another industrial union was the Mine, Mill, and Smelter Workers, but it had not made much headway.

The textile industry had a few locals scattered around the South, but so far as I can learn there was but one union agreement, in writing, in the whole industry. Indeed, there were few oral agreements, and they were of slight value in protecting the workers rights.

Though the CIO was treated, when it appeared on the scene, as a dangerous alien, most of its leadership was southern, and its members came from all the southern states. The industrial union principle—of bringing all workers in an industry or plant into one union regardless of race, religion, creed, or sex—was the only hope for organizing in the South, as it was for the mass production industries.

Whether AF of L or CIO, unions were violently resisted when they became successful. The real sin was organizing industries' employees, but the employers taught the public to call it "communism" and accused the organizers of being foreigners. I recall an instance in

19

Alabama when an Alabamian refused to join a union because its
leader was "a foreigner," but when it was revealed that the "foreigner" was born in the neighboring county, he said triumphantly—
"I knew he was a foreigner—and he was, born outside of this
county."

The United Mine Workers and the Steel Workers Organizing
Committee provided much of the leadership of the CIO in the early
days, and both had originally been in the AF of L. Some of the
AF of L craft unions also gave leaders to the newly emerging
unions. By mid-summer of 1937 CIO's SWOC had done a tremendous job in bringing tens of thousands of this vast industry's employees into the union, though there was still a tough battle ahead.
Already, in automobiles, success in General Motors and other corporations had opened the door to the final victory for the union.

Another long step in the progress of CIO had taken place in
March, 1937, when a national committee was set up to promote
organization among textile and garment workers in every branch of
the appropriate unions. Sidney Hillman, president of the Amalgamated Clothing Workers of America, had been made national director of this Textile and Garment Workers Organizing Committee.

At this time there was considerable unemployment in the South.
Many textile mills were operating on a short week of three or four
days, or less. People were hard put to live on the pittance wages
afforded by reduced employment. There was extreme poverty in the
rich city of Atlanta. Both newspapers gave good space to reporting
conditions revealed by a committee of social workers and others.

In the winter, it was a common thing to see wretchedly clothed
men and women walking through snow and sleet with guano sacking
wrapped around their feet. I remember in Columbus, Georgia, the
pitiful stories textile workers told me. Children could not go to
school in winter because they had no shoes; they could not study
their lessons because unpaid electric bills caused the power to be
cut off. I asked one man if they had oil lamps; he replied that they
had one for the family, but no money to buy kerosene. One man
told me that in the past winter the family's only green food had

been peppergrass gathered by his children along the railroad track.

There were small towns depending chiefly on the pay-roll of one mill, which might be operating only two or three days a week. Because of part-time employment, the unemployed—or partly unemployed—could not get on WPA jobs or get direct relief from the Department of Public Welfare which was administering government relief funds. When the CIO went to the heads of such federal agencies as dealt with these matters, urging supplemental aid, they were privately informed that some mill managements protested against this help, however small it was. The idea obviously was that hungry people searching for work would not be interested in joining unions.

When workers tried to form unions, employers' unfair labor practices became common—firing workers for joining unions; transferring them to undesirable jobs, and other anti-union devices were used. The unions took their cases to the National Labor Relations Board, and the Board had to take many of them to court to compel compliance with the law. By the time a worker's charges had been dragged through the courts for months, his union zeal was dampened. One federal agency head in desperation released some facts. He said that 30 per cent of the southern corporations involved were disregarding rulings of the agencies dealing with such cases. He added, "If 30 per cent of the unions involved were in non-compliance with the law and the courts there would be the devil to pay."

THE MEN AT THE TOP

These were the conditions I found when I went to work for the CIO in the summer of 1937. During the next fifteen years I was to work with a succession of able and helpful men who pushed me— often timorous of my own strength—into many rich fields of experience.

The men whose names appear in this chapter had connection with what I did, but in most instances, and from the beginning, my commission left me free to go into many situations on my own initiative, after clearing with the CIO representatives in charge.

I have already described my first official contacts with John L.

Lewis, then CIO president, and Sidney Hillman, president of the Amalgamated Clothing Workers, CIO, and chairman of the combined forces of the textile and clothing workers' unions. These were the two outstanding figures in the emerging industrial union movement of the CIO. From the time Mr. Lewis brought me into the CIO he was always fair and generous to me. I saw him from time to time, until he broke with the CIO in 1942 and I had no further contacts with him.

Sidney Hillman and I were brought in touch with each other from the time I went to New York to live. It was always a warm experience to meet him. When he smiled his whole face lit up with a friendly glow—one felt that Sidney was really glad to see one.

In his office as national chairman of the Textile Workers Organizing Committee, he had an urgently important job. In peace and war, he was one of the men in whom President Roosevelt found a tower of strength. In 1935, he was appointed one of the five members of the National Industrial Recovery Board. In 1940, he was named labor coordinator on the advisory commission to the Council of National Defense, and when the Office of Production Management was established he became associate director. In 1942 he was named head of the labor division of the War Production Board. His death in July, 1946, was a disaster, not only to the labor movement, but to the nation. I have never stopped missing him.

The only directions given me by Mr. Lewis and Mr. Hillman were to help CIO unions wherever or whenever and in whatever way I could. The nearest name to describe the job we talked of would be "roving ambassador," or "ambassador to the South." They asked me to keep them in touch with the southern situation as I saw it in my travels, to write them reports when necessary, and to see them when I might be in Washington or New York. I would be paid by James B. Carey, the secretary-treasurer of the CIO in Washington. For the present, I would use the Textile Workers' office in Atlanta.

My first act upon arriving in Atlanta was to call on Steve Nance, who was director of the CIO's southern campaign to organize workers in the textile, hosiery, and clothing industries. I had known him slightly when I began making trips to the South, promoting wage and hour legislation. He was then both president of the Georgia Federation of Labor and AF of L state legislative chairman.

Alexander Stephens Nance stood in the light and went forward as a wise and understanding leader of his time. He was not afraid to take up new issues. His life was based on principles and he had the integrity to declare them in his words and deeds.

Steve gave an immediate impression of strength and friendliness. He was tall and powerfully built, with deep-set blue eyes, a pleasant smile, and a handshake that enveloped the hand of his visitor in a warm, strong clasp. I think he was respected, trusted, and loved by more people in Atlanta than any other man.

The best description that I have of Steve Nance's motivation and character came to me shortly after his death. An old friend of his had met him on the street soon after he had resigned as president of the Georgia AF of L and gone with the CIO.

"Oh, Steve," she said, "how could you leave the AF of L for the CIO?"

"Because," he replied in a flash, "I wanted to do the most good for the greatest number of people in the shortest time."

This was a prophetic hope, for though only forty-one, Steve was to die in less than a year—on April 2, 1938—largely from overwork.

After Steve's death some of us from many circles formed a committee and printed a pamphlet in his memory, entitled "A. Steve Nance, Labor Statesman and Citizen." One of the greatest tributes in the pamphlet came from Jerome Jones, editor of the AF of L *State Journal of Labor*. I quote only a small part of Mr. Jones' editorial:

Those who knew him, and few there were in Atlanta and the State who did not know him, knew that he could subordinate his own interests to those of his fellow men more sincerely than any other person. . . . His record of leadership is more extensive, more varied and reached greater heights of personal prestige than any other active labor leader in the South. . . . Let his name be written as one who loved and served his fellow man.

In a state where politics were all too often used for personal rewards, Steve set his face against any form of benefits for himself. Twice he was offered important federal government positions that carried prestige and financial advancement. Characteristically Steve refused them both, feeling he could render greater service in the labor movement.

I have often chuckled over my meeting with Steve Nance when I reported for work at his office. It is likely that Steve recalled that meeting with some chuckles too. He had faith in the wisdom of Sidney Hillman, but I felt that he was mystified when Sidney presented to him, as one of his lieutenants, a small, white-haired, fifty-five-year-old woman who had never been in the labor movement.

Steve must have thought as we talked, "What on earth does Sidney expect me to do with this soft-voiced Virginian?" I must confess, I left Steve's office that morning equally baffled as to my part in the southern organizing drive.

Two months later, I was in Steve's office reporting on the most recent of many field trips I had made that summer. As I arose to go, spontaneously I stopped and said,

"Steve, my conscience is hurting me. You need more organizers to do the job that needs to be done. I ought to get off this staff. My salary is too high; I'm not worth it. I ought to make way for a man."

I doubt if I ever had a greater thrill run down my spine than when Steve leaned forward across the desk, focussed those intense blue eyes on mine, pointed his finger at me and said,

"Lady, you are doing a real job and don't forget it. Don't ever let me hear any more about your leaving this staff. You go places and do things the men can't do. Don't forget that one contact may be worth your salary for a whole year."

I left that office treading on air. From then on I knew that Steve and I were partners, and I knew that his doubts about me and the job had vanished.

Steve's death was a terrific blow, and his place was never really filled.

In 1939 and 1940 separate CIO directors were appointed in most of the southern states. Equally important to the southern work was the appointment of Allan S. Haywood as CIO director of organization in 1939. This was a national job of huge proportions. Mr. Haywood, among many other things, has performed outstanding services in organizing campaigns among the employees of several giant corporations.

Allan Haywood now carries the titles of director of organization, director of CIO councils, and executive vice-president. He was appointed to the last high office at the 1951 convention. This gives him broad executive authority that enables him to carry some of the burdens that formerly fell upon over-loaded Philip Murray, who had succeeded John L. Lewis as national president of the CIO.

Since Mr. Haywood was made national director of organization, I have from time to time made reports to him, and seen him in Washington. I have attended state, southern, and national conferences and conventions. Sometimes I have represented the CIO at national conferences held by various other organizations.

An important event took place in the history of the southern drive in the spring of 1946. By convention action a special Organizing Committee for the South was appointed, with a number of national unions contributing men and money.

Van A. Bittner, seasoned warrior and organizer, was appointed director of the new committee. Mr. Bittner is credited with having brought more men into unions than any other one man. It was therefore appropriate that he was given this new assignment. Like his old friends Philip Murray, Allan Haywood, and John Riffe, Mr. Bittner had begun his working life as a coal miner. One of his greatest contributions had been aiding Mr. Murray in organizing the steel empire.

Mr. Bittner set up a tightly knit organization and requested all staff men to limit their time and activities to organizing the unorgan-

ized. When the unions were strong, he said, CIO weight in politics
would count.

Mr. Bittner and I had met once for a few minutes some time
before he came to Atlanta. Whether he would want me to work on
his staff was a question I would let him decide, so I went on in my
usual way of answering calls for help and doing what should be
done. I continued to use Georgia CIO offices.

Then one Sunday afternoon at a staff meeting in Atlanta, Mr.
Bittner said the way to take care of civil rights is to have more men
with you than against you and to strike before you are struck when
the blow threatens. In reply I arose and made an impromptu statement pointing out that the safer and surer way to preserve civil
rights was to follow the procedure some of us had been using when
interfered with by sheriffs or police. This was to visit the local
authorities and point out the rights guaranteed by federal law in firm
but friendly discussion.

Next morning, Mr. Bittner's secretary called me and asked if I
could come right over to see Mr. Bittner. Said I to myself, "This is
it." But he met me cordially and said he had liked what I said at
the meeting about civil rights. He gave me a letter from Franz
Daniel, then director of the CIO in South Carolina, asking for help
in two civil rights cases involving the police and a third case involving a preacher who demanded that the textile workers choose between God and the CIO.

"Will you visit these places and see what can be done to relieve
the situations?" inquired Mr. Bittner. I said I would be happy to do
so. Returning from the trip I reported the success of the mission
in some detail to Mr. Bittner. He was pleased and asked if I would
take a special assignment on his staff to look after their civil rights
cases. From then on, whenever I narrated my most recent adventures
among the sheriffs he and I chuckled over them together.

Miss Jean B. Stultz, for seventeen years Mr. Bittner's invaluable
secretary, continues to fill an important place in the southern drive
office. She attributes the friendly relations among the CIO office staff

in Atlanta to Mr. Bittner's fine attitude and friendliness toward people. Those who are familiar with the staff would add that Miss Stultz herself has done much to bring about this happy and cooperative relationship.

Death cut off Mr. Bittner's career in the midst of its usefulness. The men associated with him on the organizing drive were bereft when he died in July, 1949. Great and powerful persons and organizations paid him a host of tributes when he was taken away from this world's labors.

For myself, I can speak of Van Bittner as I saw him and counted him my friend. He was a sincere Christian, a good citizen, an honest gentleman, a warm-hearted friend, and one who, loving his fellow men, saw the CIO as the means of bringing a better way of life to men, women, and children.

Of the many resolutions adopted in tribute to this labor-soldier, I quote two paragraphs from the finest of them:

Van A. Bittner was truly a man of the people, the working people. From the day he began to labor as a boy he dedicated to the people the work of his great heart and steady hand. He fought injustice, prejudice, exploitation and disloyalty wherever he found them and regardless of whence they stemmed.

He made justice a condition precedent to charity, and he died as he had lived in the firm conviction that only death on the battlefield can release the warrior for human rights from his service.

CIO CONVENTION OF 1950

George Baldanzi was assistant director to Mr. Bittner on the CIO Organizing Committee and was appointed by President Murray to succeed to the directorship upon Mr. Bittner's death. However, George soon resigned because he wanted to give his whole time to the Textile Workers Union of America, of which he was executive vice-president. President Emil Rieve of the Textile Workers Union then appointed James Bamford as southern director of the union. Mr. Bamford set up a southern regional office in Atlanta so that the textile workers in the South could have efficient service for their local unions. He also made possible the best cooperation between

the Textile Union staff and the southern drive staff in the job of
continuing the organization of textile workers into the CIO union.

Meanwhile, with the changes in top leadership of the southern
campaign due to Mr. Bittner's death and George Baldanzi's return
to his own union, John V. Riffe was appointed as the director by
President Murray. Mr. Riffe had worked closely with Mr. Bittner
since 1933, participating in some of the most important union victories in the coal and steel industries. He had also been assistant
to Mr. Bittner in the southern campaign.

Mr. Riffe brought a wealth of union experience to his new
responsibility. Like so many outstanding union leaders, he was a
coal miner by background and occupation. He was born March 4,
1904, and grew up in the coal mining region around Jenkins, Kentucky, going into the mines at the age of fourteen and, as he has put it
in talking to me, leading a drab and hard life. Promptly on entering
the mines he became a union member. He was in the mines sixteen
years.

For years he did volunteer organizing work in Kentucky and
Maryland. He had a hard time getting a living. He said, "I was fired
and kicked around all over the West Virginia coal mines." Promotion came in 1934 when he went to work on the UMW staff, in
District 17. After broad service as an organizer under Van Bittner,
John Riffe went on the Steel Workers Organizing Committee staff
as a sub-regional director. He participated in the Republic and
Youngstown steel strikes in Chicago in 1936—it was there that the
police massacred men and women who were attempting to form a
picket-line.

For two years, John Riffe assisted Mr. Bittner in organizing the
Bethlehem workers. When they finished they had signed their first
union contract with the second largest steel giant, and had 70,000
dues-paying members. When Mr. Bittner was assigned the task of
organizing the unorganized South, it was natural that he should
choose John V. Riffe as his associate.

Mr. Riffe, a Baptist, is a tall, fine-looking man, with blue eyes,
a ready smile, and an engaging cordiality. His son, Estes Riffe,

followed his father's example and became an organizer on the CIO staff in the South.

ROVING AMBASSADOR

These were the head men with whom I worked. At their request and always with their cooperation I have gone into the corners of the South helping the union people to achieve their aims: in organizing, in living with the law, in finding their leaders, in linking their movement to the churches, or at least getting the tolerance of the churches, in adjusting the problems of race, and creating an interest in politics. Particularly, I urged the people to keep in touch with the newspapers and to lose no chance to bring about friendly public opinion.

Strikes were among my earliest experiences in this CIO work. Unions were expanding rapidly as the National Labor Relations Act gave new and strong assistance to workers who wanted to deal with employers through collective bargaining. Embattled employers used all the means in their power to crush the new unions—and that meant legal or illegal means. CIO men were constantly calling on me to come to difficult situations. I was not an organizer, but there were many ways in which I could help organizers and local union men. Morale building was important; so I visited in workers' homes, often having meals with them, attended and spoke at meetings, walked on the picket line, and where we had a loud speaker talked to the pickets and the people on strike. I also often helped with leaflets and their distribution.

During the brief period before the federal relief agencies, including WPA, were disbanded, we occasionally got temporary jobs for the unemployed, or direct grants in food supplies.

Maintaining the civil rights of assembly, and of free speech by voice or distribution of leaflets, was an important factor to the union people, and in the process of distribution often led to arrest by sheriff or police. The heads of mills and factories regarded the sheriff and police chief as having first responsibility to keep unions out of the community. In some towns the dominant industry paid

the greater part of the police chief's salary, or made a subsidy to
the sheriff, or both. Vigilant officers of the law arrested union
representatives and ordered them to leave town. Some were jailed—
and still are, as this story will tell you—for no offence except attending a gathering where a few Negroes and many white people were
holding a union meeting. More of my time has been spent trying
to maintain the civil rights of our people than in any other one phase
of my manifold job. It has been the most exciting and interesting—
and at times dangerous—part of my life with the CIO.

The CIO has brought more hope for progress to Negroes than
any other social institution in the South—and that, sadly, includes
the church. (Among other discriminations, in white churches both
races are not admitted, and if Negroes should visit a white church
they must sit carefully segregated.) Our unions have stood four-
square for equal pay for equal work. Negroes are included in all
social security benefits, or in pension plans provided through union
contracts. Of first significance to Negroes is the acknowledgment of
themselves as persons entitled to democratic respect. Their white
brothers in the industrial unions usually succeed in convincing
Negro members that they will have not only a better living but also
more decent treatment and politeness through a CIO union.

It is a tragic fact that so far as I know *all* important efforts to
organize unions in the South—AF of L as well as CIO have
brought opposition by churches—not all churches, but enough to
be significant. Dr. Liston Pope's *Mill Hands and Preachers* tells this
story well. Management men who contribute largely to the church
and sit in the pews seem to take it as their due that mill village
preachers should throw their weight against the union. I have had
some painfully enlightening conversations with ministers of larger
churches, as well as mill churches on this subject. Even today John
Ramsay, CIO director of church and community relations, and I
are often called to towns where an evangelist or village church
preacher is attacking the CIO. This was far worse ten or fifteen
years ago, but such opposition is not altogether of the past.

In whatever job I have had I have found it wise to keep in touch with the newspapers. Thanks to this practice, I knew, from travel in the South before I came with the CIO, many editor friends, and have met many more since then. One personal illustration of the wisdom of keeping in touch with the press voices its own moral.

A few months ago, CIO representatives were trying to negotiate a contract with a well-known editor, who is with a liberal newspaper in a southern city. A sharp difference arose as to wages and the session waxed hot. The editor hastily got up and left the room. The CIO Newspaper Guildsman accused the editor of being unfair and said he would be reported to the NLRB for refusing to bargain. Upon that, the editor returned to the conference table, smiling, and said, "I am not opposed to the CIO. I have known Miss Lucy Mason for a great many years and we are good friends. She first got me to believe in the CIO." Whereupon everyone smiled, sat down, and resumed negotiations.

Though I am late in commenting on my activities in politics, this has been a field of interest to me through my adult life, beginning in Virginia and continuing into my days with the CIO. I worked for almost two years in the political field with Sidney Hillman, Paul Christopher, and others (in the background) in the two Carolinas, Georgia, Alabama, and Tennessee. That period began in 1944, when Mr. Hillman asked Allan Haywood, my chief, to allot half my time to the newly formed CIO Political Action Committee.

In one Georgia campaign, in the forties, our people had been slow in getting together on a choice for governor. One of the candidates had done a good deal of name-calling, asserting that the CIO was communistic. I was chosen to convey to him that if he would stop abusing us, we would cease attacking him. I was also to bring our people into accord on the best candidate. We wanted to keep quiet in the matter, so I got in my car and traveled north, south, east, and west, seeing union leaders—the president or the political action chairman—and telling them which was our man. The word spread quietly and quickly. Our people voted for the man we had backed, according to the election returns, but he lost because of Georgia's peculiar way of counting the ballots. The efforts of the

PAC were met by some failures, like this one, and some successes; but its importance lay in the fact that it marked the emergence of CIO into the political role which its leaders had always envisioned.

As a southern woman, aware of the burden of history, and sensitive to changing patterns in our life, I have watched for and thought about the meaning of this vigorous union movement in the South, and especially of its role as a training ground for citizenship. Watching the unions grow, as they overcome opposition, often crude violence, abuse, and misrepresentation, it delights my soul to see the constant crop of young men who come to the top and through the years become the tried and true leaders that only time and experience can make. I see in these men leaders in their communities as well as in their unions.

Chapter III

THE MOVEMENT

THE FOLLOWING chapters tell the story of the growth of the CIO in the South, as I saw it myself, or heard of it from the men and women who played leading roles. Here are stories from steel and textiles and garments and automobiles and meatpacking and rubber and wood and furniture and plastics and chemicals and a string of other southern industries. While they treat variously of unions and the workpeople and the employers, and the agencies of law and of public opinion, they have in common the hard, astonished, fast-teaching contact of labor unions and the local men of power.

My own active part in this story began with my arrival in Atlanta. I soon set about exploring the city and renewing old contacts. I also began a far-flung correspondence, breaking ground for visits later on. The day after I got to Atlanta I bought a blue Plymouth coupe. Among the cars I have owned that little coupe was the favorite—probably because it was my traveling companion in what was the most satisfying period in my life. We traveled together thirteen years and 72,000 miles.

Going about meeting union leaders and attending local union meetings, I heard about the recent automobile strike in Atlanta, and particularly about Charlie Gillman, president of the UAWA local, and leader of the successful strike, as well as chairman of a volunteer organizing committee.

As Mr. Gillman had been the man who contributed most to the

successful and peaceful nature of the strike, I called on him armed with notebook and pencils.

AUTOMOBILES: THE FIRST SIT-DOWN

Before going into his story of the strike, however, let me introduce Charlie Gillman—tall, handsome, mild-mannered Charlie, Alabama born, but taught in Georgia schools. Charlie's history is not complete until he has reminisced about his baseball career which was abruptly ended by a sprained arm. That career began when he was seventeen and in the next five years he pitched for teams in Meridian, Miss., Augusta, Ga., Spartanburg, S. C., Macon, Ga., Waterbury, Conn., and the Detroit Tigers.

After the baseball days were over, Charlie came to Atlanta and went to work in the Fisher Body plant, Atlanta Division of General Motors Corporation where he soon became active in union affairs.

When I asked Mr. Gillman to tell me the inside story of the November, 1936, strike, which had occurred eight months before I came to Atlanta, he warned me that "the only way to get anything out of me is by asking questions."

"All right," I said, "I'll wind you up with a question every time you run down."

"Just what are the full names of the two plants represented by UAW Local Union 34?"

"Chevrolet-Atlanta Division, General Motors Corporation, and Fisher Body Division Atlanta Plant, General Motors Corporation. Our union was the United Automobile Workers of America, and Local 34 represented all the employees in the two plants."

"When did you begin to organize?" I asked.

"Way back in the NRA days; we thought Section 7-A recommending that employers meet with workers in collective bargaining meant something. We took that seriously and began to organize between 1933 and 1935. But we never got anywhere with the Wolman-Bird-Kelley board that was set up to mediate differences. It did not do us any good, so we just forgot it and kept on organizing and building our union.

"The company started a company union, but that didn't get us anywhere either. As we went along the people began to realize the ineffectiveness of the company union. We became more and more interested in the real union, resulting in almost a mass joining by the men of the real union made by the workers. We began with AF of L and later went into CIO.

"This was just when the Committee for Industrial Organization was being formed, back in 1935 and '36, and an organizing drive began in the automobile industry. Nationally the Automobile Workers did not make as rapid progress as we did in Atlanta."

I asked Charlie if anything special had happened to make the men strike.

"Yes, our union was really built when management ordered George Tyson to take off his union button. I was chairman of the union bargaining committee. So Tyson and I were called in the office by Jack Roach, plant manager. Tyson was wearing his button —so was I. All our members in the upholstery or trim-line department had on CIO buttons. The plant manager said to George Tyson:

" 'You've got to take that button off or you'll be fired.' " Tyson refused to take off the button. He came over and asked my advice, and I told him to keep the button on. The plant manager told me:

" 'Unless Tyson takes off that button he'll be fired.' "

"I said, 'The fellows have a right to wear any kind of button they want to, church, or society, or union.' I told the plant manager if Tyson was fired the union would close down the plant. Then Roach said: 'Tyson is fired.'

"We left the office then and I went over to the trim-line department and told everybody as I passed by that the plant was on strike. When I got to Bill Denton, he went over and pulled the switch on the trim-line—it was right by where he was working. Then I went to the body-shop and told the fellows to stop working, that the company had fired Tyson for wearing a union button and we weren't going to work until they put him back.

"It was about noon. We had a sit-down a day and a half and one night. We sent all the women home and the men just stayed in for the day and a half. The women went to the union office and made sandwiches and coffee to bring us.

"The following day, Roach and Gallagher, the personnel director of the Chevrolet plant, came around to ask us to get the fellows out of the plant. I got up on a table and told the men to keep quiet. The men didn't want to go out. They were milling around and making a lot of noise. I felt Gallagher pulling on my pants' leg and he was saying: 'If the people will leave the plant, we will not try to operate until an agreement is reached.' All the time he was twitching my pants' leg and asking me to get the men out, and promising that the plant would stay closed."

"Then what happened?" I asked.

"The men blew off some steam, but they finally agreed that if the plant stayed closed they would leave. We set up a picket line and there was no violence and no incident to disturb us. It was a very orderly strike."

"How long were you out?"

"We were out November and December of 1936 and until the general contract was signed in 1937. We went out before I knew of any other auto plant that had gone out and we had the first sit-down strike in the auto industry.

"When Frank Murphy came in as Governor of Michigan, after the first of the year, the union in General Motors really got to work to build a union.

"Down in Atlanta we didn't have any money, we had to dig for everything to get along. We were the only local on strike at first and there weren't any other strikes in Atlanta. We surely felt lonely.

"When General Motors reached a national agreement with the United Automobile Workers of America, the obligation to bargain collectively came with the national contract. After that we had a good strong union—born on the picket line."

As Charlie recalled bit after bit of the strike, he told me that "Steve Nance advised, helped, and encouraged us in our organization and strike in every way. Steve had helped the Atlanta teachers to organize, and now he went to the Teachers Union and got thirteen hundred dollars for the kids. That money got the children toys and candy and the things that make Christmas for them. That thirteen hundred dollars Christmas money saved our strike and boosted our morale. It kept us strikers from feeling so lonely. Steve Nance was a wonderful man, never too busy to help and advise the rest of us in our union work."

In those early days, after Steve Nance's untimely death, I think Charlie Gillman more than any other one person helped to spread organization by CIO unions in the Atlanta area. He attended innumerable union meetings and gave counsel to many new union leaders. His sincerity, dignity, and cordiality made his public contacts excellent. He was asked to serve on many civic and social welfare boards and committees.

Charlie told me about the volunteer organizing committee set up by Local 34 to help organize other Atlanta workers. He was the first chairman of this group which carried the union gospel to other working men and women. This committee helped those in charge of organizing the Southern Spring Bed Company, Atlantic Steel Company, Atlanta Woolen Mills, and the people in the Cluett Peabody Arrow Shirt plant at East Point, on the edge of Atlanta.

As Gillman expressed it, "We stimulated interest and helped organize the unorganized workers. When the AF of L tried to take the Chevrolet union away from us and we won the election, we had a victory parade through the city and ended at the door of the Cluett plant. We had a loud-speaker and told the Cluett people about the union and what it meant. That victory stimulated interest and helped organize Cluett's."

Charlie Gillman was president of Local 34 from 1935 to 1939. He was elected president of the newly formed Georgia State Industrial Union Council in 1939. He was continually re-elected until 1951 when he declined to run and was succeeded by W. H. Crawford. In 1939 Mr. Gillman was appointed Georgia CIO director of organization by Allan S. Haywood, national CIO director of organization. He held the same office under the CIO Organizing Committee set up under Van A. Bittner in the spring of 1946.

We know of at least fifteen men who came out of Chevrolet Local

34 and made unions their life work. They are, besides Charlie Gillman, T. J. Starling, director District 8, UAWA; George D. Guest,
education and political action representative of UAWA, and elected
president of the Atlanta Industrial Union Council in January, 1952;
Clyde G. Brock, H. W. Denton, M. E. Duncan, T. P. Porter, Floyd
Garrett, Arthur Attaway, James Harding, Fred Pieper, Harvey Pike,
H. L. Smith, W. P. Allen, and W. T. Gillman.

There have been many changes in the automobile industry and
in the United Automobile, Aircraft, and Agricultural Implement
Workers of America, CIO, since the sit-down strike in Atlanta.
Officers of the union tell me that approximately 95 per cent of the
trucks and automobiles manufactured and assembled in the United
States and Canada are made by UAW-CIO members.

Atlanta has become an automobile center with thousands of workers. If he could recognize the makes of the cars from the sky, a man
from Mars would see Chevrolets, Fords, Buicks, Oldsmobiles, Pon-
tiacs, coming out of plants and hurrying about the streets and en-
virons of Atlanta. He would see the innumerable small, neat, and
mostly white houses that spread out from the city in all directions. In
many of them dwell auto-workers and their families.

Thomas J. Starling, for some years a local union officer, served
as steward and committeeman before following Charlie Gillman as
president of Local 34 in 1940. Since 1941 he has been director of
Region 8, southern, of the UAW.

Always curious to know how and why union leaders came into
the union in the first place and why they have continued to serve the
union, I once asked Tom Starling these questions. He first gave a
personal but valid reason—union men in the plant where he had
worked had a forty-four-hour-week and non-union men worked
forty-eight hours.

A broader outlook appeared in his second answer. "Being raised
on a farm I saw the need for raising the living standards of both
industrial and farm workers, so I became interested in the labor
movement as the best way to bring this about."

On the Road with TWOC

Charlotte

During my first summer in Atlanta, Steve Nance and I planned a long trip that began with Charlotte, North Carolina. He gave me a list of towns where the Textile Workers Organizing Committee was working, together with the names and addresses of the union representatives in charge. There was a six-weeks-old strike at Charlotte and we decided I would go directly there and then to towns in that area, working my way over to the coast.

R. R. Lawrence, executive assistant on the TWOC staff, was in charge of the strike in Charlotte. Mr. Lawrence was a seasoned union man who had formerly been president of the North Carolina Federation of Labor, and had come with the CIO early in its career.

Upon arrival I did not find anyone at the union office, so I went out to the Highland Park Mill where our union people were gathered on the picket line. I was promptly asked to make a talk over the loud-speaker that was being used to tell the workers the story of their union.

The next time I was among my old friends in Richmond, one of them gave me a vivid account of how I went to Charlotte, called all the workers out on strike, and made speeches to them on the picket line! At least, the last accusation was partly true.

Mr. Lawrence told me that the cause of the strike was the refusal of the mill management to recognize the union, or meet and bargain with its representatives.

While in Charlotte I called on the editors of the *Charlotte Observer* and *Charlotte News*. By chance my first visit was to J. E. Dowd, managing editor of the *News*. He received me with such cordiality that I was surprised. I suppose my face registered this, for he immediately said, "My wife used to be in your Sunday School class in Grace Episcopal Church in Richmond."

Before I left, Mr. Dowd conducted me around to see the other editors. Thereafter I had many contacts with some of them and

Mr. Dowd's introduction contributed to the cordial relations established. When I was leaving, Mr. Dowd commented, "You are a good advocate for the CIO." Feeling a bit flattered I asked why. Said he, "You look mild."

While in Charlotte I went to see the secretary-treasurer of the American Cotton Textile Manufacturers Association—the southern branch of the industry. I had met him several times and had talked with him in that same office in 1931, when we discussed federal regulation of hours and night work as a means of saving the cotton textile industry from over-production and improving the health of its employees.

Now, in the summer of 1937, we talked about the National Labor Relations Act. He was interested in the requirement that management "recognize the union" as the bargaining agent for its members. He was also interested in the NRA clause which had required employers "to bargain in good faith."

He wanted to know how it could be determined that an employer was refusing to bargain in good faith? What could be done to make him bargain, and how could it be determined whether he was acting in good faith? He insisted that management could actually continue indefinitely to sit at the conference table but refuse to negotiate.

In the words of this spokesman for the cotton textile industry, "Management could meet with union representatives without bargaining—forever. Furthermore, if the courts ordered the company to bargain, the company could shut down its plant, or could move the plant to another locality, even South America if necessary."

He was issuing a warning to the Textile Workers Organizing Committee—that no bargaining was to be expected. It was this attitude which finally broke the strike in Charlotte and it still predominates in the southern branch of the textile industry in 1952.

McColl and Lumberton

Leaving Charlotte, I drove to McColl and Bennettsville, S. C., neighboring towns where the five Marlboro Mills of the D. K. McColl Company were located. On May 7, 1937, a short, peaceful strike of a week or ten days had ended by negotiations between the company and union. The contract meant to the workers considerable gains in shorter hours, wages, and working conditions. It was one of the first negotiated contracts in the South.

Steve Nance, Roy Lawrence, and Ray Nixon represented the union. They were assisted in straightening out many involved wage matters by Paul R. Christopher, former textile worker and student of industrial engineering at Clemson College, who acted as technical adviser.

Myles Horton, Director of Highlander Folk School, who had offered his services as an organizer when the Textile Workers Organizing Committee got underway in the spring of 1937, was assigned to the organizing work at McColl and Bennettsville. Roy Lawrence and Ray Nixon were also with TWOC, on Mr. Nance's staff, with offices in Charlotte, N. C.

I had been asked to stop in McColl and Bennettsville principally to see Mr. D. K. McColl, president of the five mills. In my early CIO days I used to send news letters about union matters to a large number of newspaper editors. In such a letter sent out in September, 1937, I find this comment on my visit to Mr. McColl.

I talked with the head of the McColl Mill which has signed a TWOC contract. His testimony was that the union agreement was working well, that the men who negotiated the contract were honest, sensible, and reasonable, that while no production check had been made since the contract was signed, efficiency certainly had not decreased and he thought it had probably increased.

While waiting to see the mayor in McColl, I talked with a lawyer who was also awaiting his Honor. He said that unions were badly needed in the South, not only for the welfare of the working people but for the entire community, for they were the only means of raising wages and spreading buying power.

This lawyer said that Mr. McColl, the president of the Marlboro Mills, had gotten a bonus of nearly $100,000, over and above his salary, the preceding year, while the mill's employees were receiving very low wages. His comment was,

"If the workers had gotten that extra money, most of it would have been spent right here, and all the business, farms, and other enterprises would have benefited by it. When it all went into the earnings of the mill president it was not spent locally except to a small degree. The president and his family went to the big cities to buy their clothes and luxuries; and much of the special bonus money was probably invested in stocks and bonds of other industrial companies."

An editorial in Dave Clark's *Textile Bulletin,* dealt with the same subject. It reported that Mr. McColl's bonus of one-third the profits had one year yielded him $80,000. Wages the preceding year, before the union agreement, had been as low as $5.50 to $6 a week. The editorial went on to say that hours that year had been from 55 to 60 per week.

Notwithstanding the comparative ease with which the Bennettsville and McColl Mills had been organized, when contract renewal time came in December, 1937, the mills went on short time—a great money loss to the employees and hard on their families. Efforts to come to an agreement dragged on until April 2, 1938, when the mills closed down. Whether this whole process was deliberate on the part of management as the best means of discouraging organization it is not possible to prove. So far as I can learn there has not been a collective bargaining agreement involving the Marlboro Mills since 1938. Marlboro Mills is now owned by the Hesslein Company, and is called the Plymouth Manufacturing Company.

As soon as the Marlboro contract was signed, workers from Lumberton went to McColl to ask Myles Horton to come over to Lumberton and help the textile employees there to organize.

We will let Mr. Horton tell his own story.

"When I got to Lumberton in the afternoon, the committee which had come to see me at McColl met me at the hotel. We went up to my room and talked. That night I was talking to some workers brought in by the committee, who had been thinking and talking union for some time. While I was with this group in my room, a mob gathered outside my window—I was on the second floor—and told the workers they would get in trouble if they fooled around with me.

"That night, Chess Manning, one of the committee leaders and spokesman for the workers who wanted a union, had his house fired into. His wife and children were there, but nobody was hurt. Rocks were thrown through the windows of two other men who had come to see me. The little girl of one of these men was cut by flying glass and had to be taken to the doctor.

"The same night Ferman Strickland's car, which was parked in front of the hotel, had all the windows broken. Strickland was a former mill worker in Lumberton sent in by TWOC to help the Lumberton people organize.

"Until this treatment was given the people who wanted a union, no decision had been made to organize in the Mansfield and Jennings Mills in Lumberton. Next morning when I called Steve Nance to tell him what had happened, he asked what I thought should be done. I recommended that I be allowed to stay and organize as this was the only answer to such intimidation. Steve Nance agreed with me, and I went to work.

"Within a week we had signed up over one hundred members in spite of constant threats. Thanks to the encouragement of some hundred or more McColl workers, who came the thirty miles to Lumberton, it was possible to hold a public meeting. The McColl union people encouraged the Lumberton employees by telling them the story of the good relations at McColl. Some of these people had worked in the Lumberton Mills in the past.

"While waiting for the Labor Board hearing preparatory to holding an election (the first in the South after the National Labor Relations Act had been upheld by the Supreme Court), Bennett Schauffler, NLRB regional director, asked our cooperation in seeing to it that there was no strike during this trying period. The company was asked for its cooperation by ceasing to fire union people and desisting from any other form of discrimination which would have the effect of further postponing the Board hearing as new charges were filed. We gave our pledge to carry out Mr. Schauffler's wishes.

"The day before the Labor Board hearing was to start, June 7, 1937, I was notified that the workers in the Jennings Mill were out on strike. On investigation I learned that the employees had been ordered to increase their work-load fifty per cent. This, a foreman told me, would have been impossible, as the work-load was already too heavy. When the workers told the foreman that it was not possible to do more work than they were already doing, they were ordered to 'take the stretch-out, or get out.'

"It was obvious to me and to the Board's representatives that the company had deliberately forced the workers to walk out, in an effort to disrupt the discrimination hearings. Before I learned of the strike the company had requested of the Board a postponement of the hearing. This was the company's final desperate move to prevent the Board from holding hearings on the discrimination charges the union had filed against the company. The company's purpose was to break the people's morale and disrupt their union by constant postponement of the hearings.

"The workers had put their whole faith in the NLRB, which they regarded as a government agency to defend the rights of labor. The representatives of the Labor Board would not tolerate further delay on the part of the company. So the hearings were held in the county court house.

"The company began to fire people for joining the union, and also to serve eviction notices on workers who lived in company houses. It also cut off credit at the Mansfield and Jennings Company store. (H. B. Jennings was president of both these mills.)

"Of course, we filed more discrimination charges against the company with the National Labor Relations Board. In less than one month ninety per cent of the Jennings mill employees and sixty-five per cent of the Mansfield Mill people had signed union membership cards. Then we asked to meet with representatives of the company to discuss a collective bargaining agreement. This would have meant recognition of the union, and the company refused to meet with us.

"So, we filed charges with the NLRB for refusal to bargain."

There was a long war by the company on its employees at the Jennings Mill, North Lumberton, and Mansfield Mill, East Lumberton. As Don McKee reported to the *Industrial Leader,* "The industrial difficulty of the past three months in Lumberton is the story of textile employers' war to check unionization of their workers by TWOC and Myles Horton."

"The union leadership and members," Horton continued, "were not wholly friendless. More Labor Board hearings were to come. To keep up the morale of the people, union committees were developed and given responsibility for continuing to sign up workers in the two mills. These committees went out in the country arranging meetings for farmers around Lumberton where they could be told the facts about the union and their support enlisted. In each group that went out we saw that there was at least one person who know or was related to some country family they visited. As a result, large quantities of food were brought in by the farmers. At first this was a great help to the fired workers, and later when the company forced a strike it helped provide for strikers and their families.

"There were also some friendly people in the city who showed their sympathy with the union in various ways. A kindly merchant gave a vacant field for meetings and a wooden platform was built there, where mass meetings could be held.

"The workers of the Mansfield Mill walked out on a sympathy strike in support of the Jennings Mill workers who had been forced out by the company.

"The facts of the situation were as follows: For some time the management of the smaller Jennings Mill had been looking for a propitious occasion to close that mill for the purpose of installing new machinery, during which time the Jennings Mill orders would be filled by the larger Mansfield Mill. The company was trying to kill two birds with one stone by choosing this particular time to install the Jennings Mill machinery."

"The Jennings management hoped not only to prevent the hearings but to starve the Jennings workers into submission and have them return to work without a union. All of these aims could possibly have been accomplished had not the Mansfield workers come out on a sympathy strike in support of the Jennings people."

Around this time I left McColl for Lumberton, where I met John

Pate, the leader of the strikers at the Jennings Mill. It was raining
hard when I met Pate. He was tall and thin and dark haired, and
had a deep cough. I remember the rain running off his hat and down
his neck. He had a wife and three children to support. He said when
the people had gone out in an unauthorized strike against poor
working conditions and low wages, plus efforts of management to
weed out union members, "Something deep in our hearts just couldn't
stand it any longer and we walked out."

With two strikes on in a small city there was bound to be some disorder. Horton and the other TWOC representatives gave orders for
no violence and set an example by their own orderly and peaceful
conduct.

The city police were swift to carry out company requests to make
arrests among the striking union people. The fact that sixty-five
union people were *arrested* in Lumberton, on company complaints,
while *not one* union member *received a jail sentence*, is evidence
that there was no real disorder or violence on the part of union
members. The three or four small fines paid for union men were for
trespassing on company property.

Illustrative of the temper of the police toward Horton and the
union was this comment by an officer which was reported in the
Charlotte Observer of July 8, 1937:

> The officer said Myles Horton stated that he was conducting strike
> activities at the Mansfield Mills, and in view of this statement Horton
> will be arrested regardless of whether he is on the scene should any
> violence occur on the picket line, or elsewhere, concerning the strike.

This was a wide open door to arresting Horton on any excuse.

Notwithstanding the violence directed at Myles Horton and other
union people, he had refrained from attacking any one. He was
slugged and knocked to the ground several times—once by a blow
from the back. During the court trial, in which Myles was accused
of inciting a riot, David Carrol, the lawyer for the McColl and Bennettsville Mills, appeared in court and asked to be allowed to testify
as a character witness in Horton's behalf, at the request of Mr. Mc-
Coll, president of the McColl Mills.

Mr. Horton was cleared of all charges.

The Labor Board election was held September 22, 1937, and the union won by 321 against 179. The Board ordered the company to reinstate ten employees who had been discharged in May, and to reimburse them for wages lost during the period. The contract was finally entered into on January 29, 1938, and covered both the Jennings and Mansfield Mills.

The old Jennings Mill in Lumberton closed down in about 1944— that meant the death of the union there. The mill is now known as the Dennis Mill. The union in the Mansfield Mill at Lumberton is still alive and vigorous. The Mansfield Mill was bought by the Hesslein interests and now goes under the name of Caledonia Mill. An agreement with the Textile Workers Union has been in effect at the Mansfield, or Caledonia, Mill since January 1, 1938.

After I had transcribed the story of the Lumberton and McColl Mills, Joel Leighton, manager of the TWUA Joint Board in Rockingham, N. C., sent me a copy of a broadcast he made in Rockingham, November 20, 1949, part of a series entitled "The Voice of Labor." I am drawing on that script because of its references to Lumberton.

"Last Saturday night," Mr. Leighton said, "the delegates from the three local unions that have made up the South Central Board of North Carolina, Textile Workers Union of America, CIO, meeting at the Union Hall in East Rockingham, took another important step in the strengthening of the activities of the organized textile workers in this section of North Carolina."

Mr. Leighton then described the action of the Joint Board and the previous action of TWUA Local 234, Mansfield Mill, in East Lumberton, which brought about affiliation of the Mansfield local with the Joint Board. The Mansfield local, he said, was one of the oldest local unions of textile workers in North Carolina. Mr. Leighton went on:

"From now on, for administrative purposes, the workers at East Lumberton will be joined with the workers at Aleo, Pee Dee, and Wadesboro for their common good . . . to strengthen their position

for the present and to make possible greater mutual gains in the
future.

"In recognition of this important event, I asked three of the
TWUA members from Lumberton to join us here today . . . to tell
us a bit about themselves and the history of their union in Lumberton. They are Clyde Genes, president of the Mansfield Mill local;
and Horace Phillips and John Pate, both of whom are past presidents, and both of whom are now on the executive board of that
local union."

Leighton asked Clyde Genes how long he had worked at Mansfield. Genes replied, "Ever since July 5, 1938." When Joel Leighton
asked how he remembered the date so quickly, Genes said:

"For all union members, its easy to remember your employment
date, since it becomes your seniority date and is posted in your department. On the basis of that date, when a job becomes vacant, any
worker in the department is entitled to bid for the vacancy. The
person with the oldest seniority date gets the job. That is one important thing in our union contract that does away with favoritism."

Clyde was asked when he had first gone to work in textile mills.

"Thinking about that," he replied, "reminds me what a long way
we've all come since that time. That was in 1927—right here in
Rockingham."

"I don't imagine," Mr. Leighton answered, "there were many people around here that thought the day would come when not only mills
in Rockingham but mills in Lumberton and Wadesboro and other
textile centers in North Carolina would be organized."

"That first job I got was at Entwistle Mill—it's Aleo now." Clyde
Genes continued: "Then after working in the cloth room until 1932,
I learned to weave. That was in 1932 before NRA. I remember I and
other weavers at that time were working eleven hours a day, five
days a week, and making seven dollars—not seven dollars a day,
but seven dollars a week."

Joel Leighton asked Genes when he first became active in the
union at Lumberton. The answer was—"I joined right after I went

there. I began serving on the general shop committee in 1940 and became vice-president of the local union in 1947."

Horace Phillips, the next spokesman answering a question said, "My first job was right at Mansfield, filling batteries. . . . That was in 1935. Yes, sir! we made good money in those days, before the union—good money! I was making all of three cents an hour, every penny of it! I only filled batteries a little while. Then I got a good job, learning to doff. Then I tripled my pay—I jumped from three cents an hour to ten cents an hour. Of course, we worked longer hours then and so were able to make out pretty well. By working fifty-five hours I was able to make five-fifty a week."

Mr. Phillips continued: "I don't think our wages were the main reason we organized. I was working at Mansfield when we started organizing. That was in 1937. By that time I had learned to weave, and so I was making about twelve-fifty a week. I think that the *main* thing was that people just decided they wanted to have something to say about their working conditions, their jobs.

"The way it was then, for instance, the company stores took all your money. I've seen plenty of people who didn't draw a cent on payday . . . It all went to the store. If you wanted to go to a show up town, you went to the company store and got a pass. But the company store charged you for this and deducted it from your pay when payday came around. Even doctor's bills were paid through the company store."

Mr. Leighton commented: "The complete domination of people's lives in such ways is not too far in the past."

Mr. Phillips said emphatically—"And I don't want to live ever to see that day again. That's one reason why I am so strong a union member."

Joel Leighton then introduced John Pate as "the grand-daddy of this union group gathered here this day." Asked when he first went to work at Mansfield, Pate replied:

"My family moved to Lumberton in 1912. I went to work at Mansfield in 1916 as a sweeper. I made forty cents a day. We worked eleven hours a day then, five and a half days a week. That was sixty hours, two-forty a week."

In addition to being the union's first president, John Pate had served as an executive board member continuously except for one year. Joel asked Mr. Pate if he recalled some of the early times when they were organizing. John Pate answered,

"Well, that was when the CIO first started—in 1937—when an organizer came to town. He had formerly worked in Lumberton, so some of us knew him personally.

"This organizer asked some of us to meet him. We went up to the hotel where he was staying. The company had found out about his being in town, and they were having the hotel watched. Overseers, overseers' sons, and even some of the town officials were watching to see which one of us went up to the hotel. They tried to scare us, but we kept on signing up new members. It took about three months to get a majority. We had one of the first National Labor Relations Board elections in North Carolina. When the election came the union won by better than three to one."

Joel Leighton said to Mr. Pate, "You were right in the middle of the organizing work—what do you think made them organize?"

John Pate answered: "I think it was two things. Folks were fed up with going through life being afraid . . . afraid they'd lose their jobs . . . afraid they'd get out of work and their family would have a hard time. They felt that by getting all together and helping one another through a union, they could gain some security in life. I remember my own case. I was fired from the Mansfield Mill in 1928."

"What for?" asked Leighton.

"Because I voted for the wrong man for President of the United States," Pate replied. "Believe it or not, the mill officials actually watched you while you marked your ballots in those days. I voted for the wrong man, so I was fired."

Tupelo Jimmy

Where Jimmy Cox and I first met, I don't remember. It was in August of my first summer with the CIO. We must have met in

Atlanta or in some union gathering where he had gone looking for help. The meeting resulted in my driving to the small city of Tupelo, Mississippi, in the heart of Congressman John E. Rankin's territory.

Jimmy was a worker in a run-down, obsolete, small cotton mill in bad financial shape. The mill had been deteriorating for some time, I was told. Its stockholders had not received dividends for a long time. The commission man who handled selling the mill's goods was the only one connected with the plant who made any money on it— it was said he had bought the mill and got his profit out of commissions for selling its goods. It seemed about the worst possible place to try to organize.

Jimmy knew that the CIO was doing a lot for southern workers, and he did not know anything about the finances of that little mill. He thought that if only a union could be organized the situation could be worked out. Wages and working conditions were bad— there was plenty to make the people desperate and ready to try anything. The result was a strike which took most of the people out of the plant, but was now disintegrating. The owner closed the mill. Some of the people drifted away to try their luck elsewhere.

Townspeople spread the rumor that if Jimmy could be gotten rid of the strike would end, the mill open, and people go back to work.

The background in Tupelo was most unfavorable for labor unions. Congressman Rankin had worked hard for the Tennessee Valley Authority for the simple reason that it meant cheap electric power for his own town and state—he wanted industries for Tupelo. He had fought every piece of progressive labor legislation promoted by the New Deal. The National Labor Relations Act had aroused his utmost fury and he had said that if it became law the streets of southern towns would run red with blood. He failed to say that if blood was shed, it would be the blood of the workers—not that of management, police, or the public.

There was a garment plant in Tupelo that made women's garments and the employees had become interested in a union. Up in Memphis, what newspapers called "a society girl," Ida Sledge, social worker by training, helped in efforts to organize a local union of the

International Ladies Garment Workers. Somehow the garment workers in Tupelo heard about her and asked her to come help them. It resulted in Ida's going to Tupelo to organize the women garment workers into the International Ladies Garment Workers Union.

Already I had heard of Ida's adventures. Her first was an early-morning visit in her hotel room from a number of women from the garment factory, whom the management had persuaded to form a small mob when the morning shift came on. They made her hustle into her clothes and walked her out of town, all the while threatening her with her life if she came back. Later in the day Ida returned to the hotel.

A few days later a delegation of "best citizens"—young men from the social and business circles of Tupelo—entered her hotel room at night. When she tried to use the phone to get a newspaper friend in Memphis, she was told the wires were disconnected. Again she had to hustle into her clothes, fling the rest into a suitcase, and get out. This crowd took her to the railroad station and saw that she took the next train—with dire warnings as to what would happen if she came back.

(During this time I had been on my way to Tupelo in my blue coupe.)

Strangers were not welcome in Tupelo. At the post office I got out to inquire my way to the street number that meant Jimmy's home in the mill village. The dignified, elderly man to whom I spoke gave me a suspicious and hostile look.

Ida was sleeping across town in the spare room of a nice young couple. She used part of a room in Jimmy's house for her office, with her typewriter on top of a trunk. When I arrived I saw that the house was in wretched condition, had but two fair-sized rooms, a tiny back porch with running water—no bath. The bedroom had two double beds, the other room was kitchen, sitting room, and storeroom. Furnishings were sparse. The family made me have the evening meal with them and I observed that Ida brought along a good part of it.

Excitement began late Saturday afternoon. There was a special meeting of the cotton mill union people, from which Jimmy returned to tell us that the people had voted to continue the strike. Within an hour the village was rife with rumors that a mob was going to take Jimmy out and hang him that night. Union men came to warn him to leave town. A friend brought him a pistol, which I persuaded him to return—since it was a sure way to suicide for Jimmy to be seen handling a pistol.

I tried to see Claude Clayton, city attorney, but his mother told me he had gone fishing and would not be back until midnight. I left a note to him with her, in which I urged his help. I had never met Mr. Clayton, but Ida and Jimmy believed he would take steps to protect them if he could be found. He had warned Tupelo's best citizens that if any one interfered with her again he would go to all limits in prosecuting, "let the chips fall where they may."

Next day, Sunday morning, I found Mr. Clayton at home and we had a long talk. It seemed that when he got in late the night before he read my note and went straight to the chief of police. Special officers were put on around the mill village. But the night was quiet. Mr. Clayton thought the attacks on Jimmy and Ida were over.

Saturday night, Ida and the two sweet little girls and I stayed at the home where Ida had a room. Jimmy wanted to stay at his home and face the enemy alone, but I told him that if he did, I would sit up all night on the front porch. That was too much for his chivalrous soul and we got him off to the home of friends.

About two weeks later, I had a wire from Ida saying that a group of men from the garment plant (instigated by the employer of course) had picked up Jimmy on the street and taken him out into the country on a lonely road. They said they were going to drag him to death, tied to the car's rear axle.

They actually put the rope around his neck. They beat and kicked him so badly he had to go to a hospital for some days. Jimmy had a fluent tongue and believed in his cause. He asked to be heard before they killed him, and whether from conscience or from fear of the law, they let him go after he promised not to return to Tupelo.

Help to Huntsville

Huntsville is a pretty little North Alabama town, set in a green and rolling country, not far from Tupelo. Its chief industry is textiles, and at times there have been four mills operating, with a total of several thousand employees. I have never had a chance to see its "social and cultural life"—for my frequent encounters with the editor of the *Huntsville Times* could hardly be called on the social side.

Whenever I was suddenly called to Huntsville because of some emergency situation, it was a question of getting there as fast as I could, spending my time with the local union people and the representatives of TWOC, and seeing some of the citizens the union people wanted me to talk with. Then I would go back by Birmingham and spend some time with the newspaper editors on the subject of conditions at Huntsville and the progress of CIO unions in the South.

Because of events which took place in connection with the Dallas and Merrimack Mills, they are the subject of this story, without reference to the other two mills in Huntsville with which things were going quietly.

Some of the local unions in Huntsville had been there for several years before the general cotton textile strike in 1934. They were among the oldest locals in the South—but they did not have written and signed collective bargaining agreements arrived at by negotiation. Indeed, it seems to have been some advance when management would sit down across the table and admit that the union representatives did in truth represent the union workers. Recognition was the first step, negotiation—or discussion of all points—the second, and a written, signed agreement the third. Probably the struggle between union and management in these two cases was greatly aggravated by the lack of any defined and signed contract between the parties. The first real contract with the Dallas Mill came in October, 1938, and with Merrimack several months later.

The Dallas Mill was part of a chain of twenty-one mills when this story began. Steve Nance had negotiated a verbal agreement in the spring of 1937. That summer the company got the Roper Company, a firm of efficiency engineers, to make a study which resulted in eliminating a great many people, increasing the work-load for those employees who remained, and cutting real wages.

The new agreement terms and their actual effect on the workers caused considerable altercation. Finally the mill closed in November, 1937, and remained closed until around the first of April, 1938, when management wanted to open it. But instead of calling back the workers who had been in the mill when it closed (most of them union members) management claimed they had no employees; that the November dismissal was permanent. The Mill management requested the State Employment Service to supply the needed workers. The union insisted that the former workers, as members of the union, had an agreement with the mill when it closed and should be called back. But the company stood firm.

Naturally, a strike was called by the union which picketed the mill to keep the new people out. The Dallas manager was a man from Georgia, said to be hard and bitter against the union. Some of the citizens of Huntsville were enlisted on the side of management in trying to break the union.

A citizens' committee was formed and one of the most active opponents of the union was the editor of *The Huntsville Times*. In April, 1938, the editor threatened the union people that the mills would move away, and that they would find themselves black-listed wherever they went. I quote a few lines from one of these editorials:

You may go to Chattanooga or Birmingham, New York or Chicago, BUT THERE ARE NO JOBS THERE FOR YOU. . . . If application is made to another mill elsewhere, the story of this city will be familiar, until your dying days!

I used to see this editor when I went to Huntsville—he was always personally polite, but I never saw a more acid person than he was when he talked of unions. He used to call the TWOC a snake and said it must be killed at once and never allowed to raise its head again.

As the deadlock continued, the Dallas management announced they were going to open the mill and start work. The union replied that it would picket the mill to see that only former employees went in. Management then asked the Governor to send in militia to protect the new employees and get them into the mill. The Governor said the trouble should be settled by conciliation and arbitration, which was his consistent stand during the altercation. The union also demanded arbitration, with Governor Graves as the arbitrator. The company flatly refused to be a party to arbitration, saying they would stand on their right to employ whom they wanted.

Suddenly the citizens' committee announced that a cavalcade of automobiles would leave Huntsville on April 20 and proceed to the Governor's office in Montgomery to petition him to send troops to Huntsville and break the strike. At this point, Roy Lawrence called me up and asked me to go at once to Huntsville.

But before going to Huntsville I went to Birmingham, arriving by train on the morning of the nineteenth and proceeding at once to the editorial office of the *Age-Herald*. Then I was with editors of *The News* and finally of the *Post*. I began at the top but was careful to see the next top man in each case. All three papers had been having heavily slanted editorials in favor of sending militia to open the mill.

My total talking time in these editorial offices was just over six hours in one day, and I was armed with a long column containing my story of the situation in the Dallas Mill. The *Age-Herald* printed that in full. Next day those three papers had strong appeals for what the union had asked loud and long—"conciliation and arbitration." I got the same favorable editorial slant from the *Montgomery Advertiser*—by long distance telephone call. That was the best job in changing editors' opinions that ever I did.

Next morning, Bill Mitch, then state director of the CIO, drove me in his car to Huntsville. We met the citizens' cavalcade enroute to Montgomery—horns blowing, men shouting and already triumphant. But they went home very flat, very quiet—we met them straggling back, their line of march all broken. The Governor had given

them a courteous reception—offered conciliation and arbitration—
at which the unruly crowd had shouted and jeered and booed.

In due time the Dallas mill opened and the union had not been
killed.

Meanwhile, some time in 1938 the Textile Workers Organizing
Committee had negotiated an agreement with the Merrimack Mill.
Borden Burr, the mill attorney, however, had been successful in
keeping the management from signing, so there was no contract.
When this verbal agreement expired there was a long strike. It lasted
more than a year and caused great suffering among the people.

When cold weather came in the winter of 1938, the Merrimack
Mill continued its severe policy of evicting mill village workers, putting them out in groups. I have before me a "Partial Report on Eviction Survey, Merrimack Mill Village, November 19, 1938," made by
the "Women's Emergency Committee on Evictions and Welfare."

This committee personally canvassed the situation. There was an
incredible amount of destitution, overcrowding, and undernourish-
ment. One house with four rooms contained fifteen people, with four
beds for all of them. A man with a daughter near death in the hospital requested a few days' postponement of eviction, but was refused. The girl died the day the family was evicted.

The report showed that real estate and business interests were involved in a widespread conspiracy to drive the evicted people out of
the community—yet the workers' average time of employment in
the mill was fourteen years per person. The families had lived from
two to twenty-three years in the houses from which they were evicted.

I was in Birmingham November 23, 1938, to hear Mrs. Roosevelt
speak in the city auditorium to the Southern Conference for Human
Welfare. The Merrimack local appointed a delegation to attend this
conference, hoping that Mrs. Roosevelt would tell the President of
their plight. Late that afternoon, Roy Lawrence asked me to meet with
him and the Huntsville delegation. We had a conference and decided
to try to ask Mrs. Roosevelt to meet us right after the address, before
she left for her night train to Warm Springs. She would be with the
President in the morning.

Mrs. Roosevelt had many appointments and I could not find her until she had gone on the platform where she would speak. So I wrote her a note, asking if she would meet with the delegation, Roy, and me, in the rear, left wing of the platform as soon as the meeting was over. I told her where I would be standing, when she read my note.

I waited until the question period, then sent my note in when it would be one of many coming to Mrs. Roosevelt. Characteristically, she looked up and in an instant our eyes met and she smiled and nodded yes. When the meeting was over I ran up to her and we went to the left wing, with a mob trying to follow us. When the police understood the situation they helped us and we joined hands to make a circle around Mrs. Roosevelt, so that it would be possible for the Huntsville men to tell their tragic story.

I'll never forget that sight. Mrs. Roosevelt, tall, lovely, gracious, shaking each work-hardened hand and bending her head to catch what each man said. They made their requests—for army tents for shelter to keep their families from sleeping outdoors, investigation of their plight, and aid from federal agencies. To all, Mrs. Roosevelt said, "I don't know what the President can do. I will tell him all you have told me. I know he will do what he can, but remember there are many limits to his power to help."

Then when she swung away from the group to go to her train, she caught my arm in hers and while I apologized for asking her time and attention, she said it was all right, and that she only hoped the President could devise something when she told him the situation.

Next morning, Thanksgiving Day, I drove back to Huntsville with Yelverton Cowherd, Dr. Witherspoon Dodge, of the TWOC staff, and Bill Mitch. We gathered in the hotel room of one of the men and discussed further steps. Union men crowded in and out. They were elated over Mrs. Roosevelt's promise to take this story to the President.

Paul Styles, a field investigator for the National Labor Relations Board, came in and told us that he had been called from the NLRB office that morning and told to go at once to Huntsville. The message said the President had that morning requested the NLRB top office in Washington and the Department of Labor to send investigators immediately into Huntsville in order that they might inform him of the situation there as quickly as possible.

It happened that two conciliators from the Department of Labor and Styles from the Regional NLRB had actually been in Huntsville when these orders came, because the crucial nature of the situation had led to their being assigned there during the emergency. Paul Styles was a native of Huntsville.

The personal appeal to Mrs. Roosevelt—her report to the President and his immediate action—greatly aided the Merrimack people. The evictions immediately stopped, relief was given, and it became possible for the National TWOC to rent an empty hotel for the evicted families. In the end a contract was secured.

The manager of the Merrimack Mill told a Conciliation Bureau representative that "if everybody had stayed out of Huntsville" he could have handled the situation by evicting the people, who would then have left Huntsville. This man had boasted of gettting rid of "undesirable workers" (union members) by similar methods in Gastonia, North Carolina, some years before.

This "everybody" who had interfered with his plan, of course, included the President of the United States and his wife.

COAL FIRST

It is impossible to talk about the development of the United Steelworkers of America in Alabama, or, for that matter, in the South, without also talking about the United Mine Workers of America.

When the CIO was formed, the United Mine Workers was among the foremost unions, for it had already been organized and functioning as an industrial union for many years. Many leaders in the United Steelworkers were once coal miners and leaders in the UMW.

The United Mine Workers had taken full advantage of the collective bargaining clause of the NRA when that agency went into operation in the summer of 1933. A fine illustration of this was in Alabama where William Mitch was sent early in June, 1933, to direct the organizing campaign of UMW, District 20, an office he filled so well that in a short time nearly all the miners in the area were members of the UMW. The only exceptions were a few miners in isolated sections and some small truck mines. Strenuous efforts were made by strong captive-mining companies (who use their own coal in steel making) to oppose unionization of the coal miners they employed. Then they, too, were finally obliged to sign the UMW collective bargaining agreement.

When the United Mine Workers withdrew from the CIO in 1942, the character and integrity of William Mitch, and his devotion to labor union principles, had endeared him to so many union people that a warm friendship still continues between him and many of us in the CIO.

Since I played no part in this story, I asked William Mitch to give me some facts about early organization in Alabama, as well as an up-to-date account of UMW history and the formation of SWOC in Alabama. What follows is taken from Mr. Mitch's account. By request, he begins and ends his story with an autobiographical sketch.

"I started work in the coal mines of Ohio, Indiana, and Illinois, and was selected as traveling auditor in 1912. In 1913, I was elected secretary-treasurer of District 11, Indiana, of UMWA, and served sixteen consecutive years, being elected each year by referendum vote.

"In 1929, I was selected as an international representative of the UMWA. I did organizing work in Illinois, Indiana, Kentucky, and West Virginia, and by the way, while I was in northern West Virginia, Van A. Bittner was in charge of the district, with headquarters at Fairmont, West Virginia.

"I was sent to Alabama just before the NRA became a law, and started our campaign of organization. I was designated as president of District 20, and international representative of the UMWA. At that time there was not one member of the United Mine Workers of America in Alabama, District 20.

"It was a real problem because prior organization of the UMWA locals followed the old southern tradition—with the white workers in one local and the colored in another. Our position was that they should all be in the same local, and with this in view we perfected our organization.

"The colored workers were very responsive and anxious, as a rule, to become members of the United Mine Workers of America, and most of the white workers were likewise.

"We started our campaign of organization in Alabama on June 5, 1933. It was a whirlwind campaign. On July 20, 1933, we held the largest labor convention ever held in Alabama. At that time the mine workers economically were in deplorable circumstances. They came to that meeting in trucks, haywagons, and any other vehicle they could find, from all over the state. They were then working from nine to fifteen hours a day, and were receiving about $1.50 per day.

"There were no rules governing representation at that convention. The locals sent as many representatives as they desired. We filled the Birmingham City Auditorium to capacity. The workers were anxious for an organization because financially they were at a low ebb.

"When the United Mine Workers, through John L. Lewis, started the campaign to organize the CIO, along with representatives of other organizations, many of them still affiliated, I was selected at state president of the CIO. Just prior to that, I had served the workers in Alabama as president of the Alabama State Federation of Labor (AF of L).

"Later the campaign was started to organize steel. Philip Murray, then vice-president of the United Mine Workers, was placed in charge. I was selected as SWOC regional director for the South. Van A. Bittner and Clinton Golden were selected as directors of the northern, eastern, and western sections of the United States. We were instrumental, in a great measure, in inaugurating the initial activities affecting the organization of the steelworkers, then known as the Steel Workers Organizing Committee. I selected Noel R. Beddow as assistant director in Steel, who worked with me for a number of years in this capacity, and was a real asset. Yelverton Cowherd served most of the time in a general cooperative way, and was later selected as secretary of the CIO in the state of Alabama, being elected at various conventions. Of course, our activities in the CIO organizational campaign took us into various activities covering coal, iron ore, steel, textile, and many others.

"I moved my membership to the First Methodist Church of Birmingham when I came here, and have been a member ever since.

"As to my hobbies, well, I like to play golf, but more as an exercise than as a hobby. Painting, both oil and water colors, and drawing (pen and ink work) have been definite hobbies for many years."

Mr. Mitch has a fine son. Young Bill is a lawyer and, as one would expect, a labor lawyer. The Birmingham law office in which he works has an interesting combination of personalities. Its three lawyers are Jerome Cooper, CIO counsel in the South; William Mitch, Jr., counsel for the United Mine Workers; and young Hugo Black, son of the Supreme Court Justice, and also specializing in labor law.

Steel—the Beginning

The greatest single CIO victory in the South was the organization of the Tennessee Coal and Iron Company employees in the Birmingham area. This was automatically accomplished when the United States Steel Corporation, owner of TCI, signed a collective bargaining agreement with SWOC in March, 1937. More than 20,000 steel workers in Birmingham and its suburbs were included in the 125,000 employees of the Steel Corporation now under union-management agreement.

Because that victory was of such vital significance to the steelworkers and to the whole area it is relevant to give a sketch of SWOC's background here, although, again, I cannot report it firsthand. The Alabama and Bessemer Twelfth Convention Report had a brief history of the United Steelworkers and I am lifting out part of that story for use here:

Open discrimination, violations of civil rights and other forms of persecution and intimidation have been historically identified with the steel industry. . . . Beginning in the 1870's, when the first inadequate attempts to organize were made, the steelworkers were split one against the other along occupational, racial, religious and nationality lines. . . .

The era was marked by brutal murders, industrial espionage and black-listing. Feudalism ruled steel towns and communities throughout the early days.

Union organization was met with vicious attacks against those who dared to talk "union." The pages of history are full of the bitter struggle, the bloodshed, the outright killings of union men, the use of tear gas, company police and ruthless intimidation.

The twelve men who sat in an office on the twelfth floor of a building in downtown Pittsburgh on a hot summer day in June, 1936, knew what they were facing.

Homestead 1892! The steel strikes of 1909 and 1919! Martial law! Tear gas! The power and wealth and might of an industry which had relentlessly fought unionism through the years. . . .

In between the formation of the Committee for Industrial Organization (later changed to the Congress of Industrial Organizations) and its expulsion by the AFofL, there was formed in the spring of 1936, the Steel Workers Organizing Committee. It was one of several such committees designed to organize the mass-production industries which the AFofL had so long neglected.

Philip Murray was named chairman of the newly-created SWOC. Others that helped launch the SWOC were Van A. Bittner, representing the United Mine Workers; Clinton S. Golden, who was named as eastern regional director; David J. McDonald, chosen secretary-treasurer; and other representatives of the following organizations: the Amalgamated Association of Iron, Steel, and Tin Workers; the International Ladies Garment Workers; and the Amalgamated Clothing Workers.

The twelve men sat down to map the steel organizing campaign. They established national headquarters in Pittsburgh, a regional office in Chicago, one in the East and another in the South in Birmingham.

Steel, the Verdun of the American Labor Movement, was now enthusiastically tackled. . . .

Just two weeks after the campaign got under way, the American Iron and Steel Institute threw down a challenge. The Institute bought full page advertisements in 375 metropolitan newspapers, at an expenditure of around $500,000, to appeal to the "public and the employees in the steel industry."

It is interesting to observe that SWOC set out to organize the steel industry with $500,000, while the industry, in one advertisement, spent that much to block the drive! . . . When SWOC failed to fold up under the summer blasts of an angry industry . . . the four chief weapons of anti-unionism were invoked—as revealed years later by the LaFollette

Committee which was created to investigate violations of the right of free speech and assembly and interference with the right of labor to organize and bargain collectively. They were: Strikebreaking, industrial espionage, private police systems and industrial munitions.

Steel was girding for a war on unionism. One of the first moves planned in the campaign of SWOC was to "capture" company unions. It was apparent that many of these Employee Representation Plan leaders wanted a legitimate union.

The next paragraphs of the SWOC story reported the wholesale movement to scrap Employee Representation plans and form real local unions in the Steel Workers Organizing Committee. The article said, "Steelworkers began joining at the rate of 2,000 daily." To turn back to the report from which this story is taken—

It was in March, 1937, that reporters from all parts of the nation came to Pittsburgh to hear announcement of a steel strike. Instead, however, they spotted Chairman Murray and a committee walking into a Pittsburgh skyscraper. The wires sped the news across the nation. United States Steel had signed a contract with the Steel Workers Organizing Committee! The $5. a day minimum wage was won for about 175,000 steel workers in the first genuine collective bargaining agreement achieved in the basic steel industry. It was a stirring day in labor history. . . .

The USA-CIO today has more than one million members, with more than 30,000 members in District 36.

In its steady, unceasing, forward fight, the USA-CIO has raised wages in the industry to the highest levels in history, has established the first non-contributory pension system, adequate social insurance program, liberal vacations with pay, paid holidays, streamlined grievance procedure and countless other benefits that have given all steel workers a full measure of industrial participation.

Today Philip Murray, President of a million steelworkers, and of many more millions of CIO members, leads more men than probably any other union officer. I am thankful to know Phil Murray. His virtues as a citizen, a churchman, and a friend and his abilities as an organizer, negotiator, and union leader are too well known to need recitation here. His greatest concern is to serve his fellow men and make life better worth living for the men, women, and children in American families.

With all his powers, it is inspiring to see so great, so wise, and so good a man remain essentially modest and close to the working people he represents. Phil Murray cares for men's souls as well as their economic needs. He combines loyalty to his religion with the traits of a truly great labor statesman and a wise and loyal citizen.

THE CLOTHING WORKERS AMALGAMATE

Another union which had appeared on the southern scene in the early days of the CIO was the Amalgamated Clothing Workers of America. Already in 1935 a contract had been negotiated at Fried-man-Harry Marks in Richmond, Virginia, which was to be significant because it was Amalgamated's first contract that became lasting in the South. It was also one of the three cases in which the National Labor Relations Act was upheld by the Supreme Court of the United States.

The man who had organized the workers at Friedman-Harry Marks was the Reverend Charles Webber, and his story is told in the chapter on "The Church." One of my more exciting experiences in the Amalgamated's service began a few years later with a letter from Bernard Borah, southern director for this union.

"Our organizers have been driven out of Blank three times," wrote Borah. "The last time, Ed Blair was taken out of his hotel by a mob of citizens and warned not to come back lest he get much worse treatment." He went on to say that the third time he had sent in a woman, Mrs. Eula McGill, but she fared no better. The mob went to her hotel room, made her pack hastily, and told her to get out and stay out, or it would be hard for her. My good young friend, with whom I had worked in many situations, ended his letter, "I wish you would go in there and see what can be done."

So I set forth in my Plymouth as soon as possible. Upon arrival I parked my car in front of the courthouse and went across the street to see the bank president. It was he who had taken leadership in fighting organization of the town's recently built garment factory.

The tall, handsome young banker was in the cashier's cage and as I approached he gave me a friendly greeting—probably mistaking me for a new depositor. We talked about the lovely country and the weather and how I had enjoyed my drive. I confided that my brother-in-law was a bank president in Alexandria, Virginia. When I told him my occupation the transformation was instantaneous. His smile froze, the muscles of his face tightened—enmity replaced cordiality.

"We don't want the CIO around here," he said, and proceeded to tell me what he thought of the CIO and all its unions, works, and ways. I reminded him of federal laws, such as the National Labor Relations Act, which guaranteed the right of workers to organize, and also the rights of free assembly and free speech. All of this was piffle to the banker.

"If the government in Washington under this crazy New Deal passes laws that this town disapproves, the thing for us and other towns to do is to ignore them," he declared. "We are law-abiding people in this country, we don't need any police to protect us. We sleep with our doors open, but we have a pistol on the table beside our bed and know how to use it. Vigilantes perform a useful service and are often brave and effective men."

"We don't know anything about civil rights," the banker continued, "but we know how to protect our own rights. The Labor Board is unfair and should be disregarded until Congress wipes it out."

Though I went at once to call on the judge (also on the anti-union committee) the banker must have already phoned him, for he was looking suspicious. When I told him my mission, the judge pounded his desk and said, "I'm not going to talk to anybody about this damned CIO. I am against it and am going to do all I can to get it out of here." He hurried into another room and banged the door behind him.

So I went to the mayor's office—but he was in the state capitol many miles away. I had good luck in his office for I found his brother, an intelligent young lawyer who knew the need for unions, and had been counsel for farmers' cooperatives in that region. He told me what I suspected already. The town had given a substantial subsidy to the northern company that built the garment factory. He did not think the union could get anywhere until a large addition to the plant was completed and paid for.

While we were talking the telephone rang and I could hear the judge's voice roaring out the story of my visits to him and the banker. He wanted to ask the mayor what could be done about my presence in town. My friend told the judge that he saw no occasion for alarm over my being there, and as a lawyer he thought there was nothing the judge or others could do about it—also that he thought I would not be there long. When he put down the telephone he shook his head and smiled at me.

The young man advised me not to be in town when night fell, but well on the way to my destination. He did not think the citizens' committee would interfere with me, but tension was high and you could not tell what might happen.

The newspaper editor was away, but I talked with two of his associates. Later I had a letter from a fine young Methodist minister who regretted that I had not discovered him as he was unhappy about the lawless behavior of the citizens' committee. Nevertheless, I was forced to write this visit down as one of my less successful ventures.

Shirts and Collars

One of the first CIO unions strongly established in Atlanta was among the employees in Cluett Peabody & Company. This company is famous for Arrow brand shirts and collars.

The successful Automobile Workers strike in 1935 had been a great stimulus to organizing the Cluett plant. Charlie Gillman, chairman of the autoworkers organizing committee, took an active part and I saw him often at Cluett local meetings.

Bernard Borah, and May Bagwell also of the Amalgamated staff, spent much time in helping organize the workers, and I often worked with them. The KKK was active in opposition. A cross was burnt in a union member's yard. Sometimes when I was speaking at a union meeting, Klansmen drove by in their robes, honking their horns.

When the company proved intractable and would not yield to the union in matters of great concern to it, an arbitrator was called in, but he did not succeed in finding a meeting ground.

Under such circumstances a strike was almost inevitable. The walk-out occurred in 1941 and lasted nearly two weeks. When the Atlanta girls walked out, the workers in the northern plants followed suit and almost overnight Cluett Peabody & Company found itself involved in a company-wide strike. During the negotiations a committee of women from the Atlanta plant went to Troy to take part in negotiations. After that it took only a few days for company and union to get together, and the Atlanta committee came home triumphantly bearing the Cluett and Peabody's first general collective bargaining contract with the workers. Today, the relations between this large company and the clothing workers union are excellent.

At the time of the strike Mrs. Leora Barfield was president of the local, an office she filled for several years. She is now business agent and manager for the Atlanta local, and manager of the North Georgia Joint Board, which includes Bremen and Buchanan. There are approximately 1500 union members in this group.

Since its early days in the South, the Amalgamated Clothing Workers has piled up organizing victories in this region. Dr. Gladys Dickason, vice-president of the ACWA and especially responsible for the southern states, has sent me a long and detailed account of the present encouraging situation, and the names of organized companies look like a clothing manufacturer's catalogue. In the following, reference is made only to larger plants located in the South.

The widely known Arrow brand shirts, collars, neckties, and sport goods are made by 9000 union people employed in Cluett Peabody and Company plants, north and south.

Men's and boys' clothing manufactured by the Palm Beach Company are all southern made (except for one cutting room in Cincinnati) with more than 2500 employees in the company's seven plants in four southern states, including Alabama, South Carolina, Tennessee, and Kentucky.

Nearly 1000 workers in the South are covered by agreements with the Manhattan Shirt Company, which has a large plant at Americus, Georgia.

Some of these clothing manufacturers are located entirely in the South. As I write, I see Haspel Brothers' name. This company has only two plants, with about 1000 workers—one in Tylertown, Mississippi, and the other in New Orleans.

Amalgamated work and sport shirts, work pants and pajamas are made by the Reliance Manufacturing Company with about 1750 employees in Montgomery, Alabama, and in Laurel and Hattiesburg, Mississippi.

Merit Clothing Company in Mayfield, Kentucky, with some 2000 workers in its only plant, is under contract with the Amalgamated Clothing Workers.

Familiar brand and company names are on every page of Dr. Dickason's long letter. She says:

"We now have locals in every southern state," and continues:

Another point of interest about Amalgamated organization in the South is that most of the locals are situated in relatively small towns. A large proportion of the members, therefore, comes from farms. The point of this is that the labor movement is reaching out into the small towns and rural areas and is not being concentrated solely in large cities. . . .

The way is still difficult; citizens' committees work against the union, union people are discharged in violation of the law, and so forth, but a strong foundation has been laid. In numbers of communities when the garment factory is the sole or leading manufacturing enterprise, local business men speak quite freely of the improvement in business *after* the unionization of the plant.

COPPER MINERS OF DUCKTOWN

In the summer of 1938, Dick Anderson of the Mine, Mill & Smelter Workers (then CIO), appeared at the CIO offices in Atlanta and asked for public relations help at Ducktown, Tennessee. There was a strike by the copper miners on the Ducktown side of the stream, but the men in the smelting plant on the Copperhill side were AF of L members. I had to attend a meeting at Highlander Folk School and promised to drive on from there through Cleveland, Tennessee, to Ducktown.

After a late getaway from Highlander I arrived at the end of the

hard finished road at Cleveland at night fall. My road on to Ducktown ran close to the little river that flows between Copperhill and
Ducktown. I did not know that the fairly broad stream on my right
was only a few inches deep. The winding road kept me hugging
the outside track and the river was uncomfortably close as I took
the sharp curves in the dark.

Arriving on top of the mountain, I was soon in Ducktown and
found the hotel. There Anderson was waiting for me and we went
to my room to talk things over and give me a picture of the situation
so that I could go right to work the next morning. Anderson had a
list of persons he wanted me to talk with, mostly in Copperhill,
which was much more of a town than I had expected.

The most sensible and fair person I met in Copperhill was a
prominent doctor. He told me about the copper mines and the high
death rate of the miners with what the townspeople called "miners'
tuberculosis." Really a form of silicosis. The doctor was righteously
indignant over the bad conditions of the mines leading to a shock-
ingly high death rate. He wanted the miners to organize so that they
could collectively secure better working conditions. There was no
hope any other way.

The doctor gave me some names, some of whose owners I saw
and found friendly. Some I could not find and others were antagonistic and could see only dangerous devils in the CIO. The silicosis
they shrugged off—it always had been that way and always would be.

At the Copperhill furniture store I saw an unusual sight—coffins
were lined up on one side of the store. I expressed surprise at this
unusual combination of furniture and coffins in the front part of a
store. "Well," said the proprietor without any resentment, "these men
need coffins more than anything else because of the miners' tuberculosis—it is mighty bad around the mines."

Someone told me the druggist might be sympathetic since he had
the opportunity to know how devastating the "miners' tuberculosis"
was. But when the druggist stepped forward cheerfully and I told
him my reason for being there, he turned and hurried up the back
steps. The next man I saw was friendly and told me that the druggist

and other leading business men were, at the time of my call, meeting upstairs in the drugstore to decide what they could do to keep the CIO out of the mines.

To anyone who has never seen the devastated valley between the two small cities it is hard to visualize the raw, red earth, the shallow little river wandering between the hillocks of mud in its bed, and the lack of green anywhere. It was fumes from an earlier smelting process which, by destroying all vegetation, had caused the special desolation of the Copperhill-Ducktown area.

Late in the afternoon I went back to the hotel and Anderson took me to a union meeting. I can still see the thin, yellow faces and sunken chests of men whose lives were eaten away each day as they worked.

The striking miners were greatly in need of food. I promised to try to get a carload of surplus products to carry them through the immediate situation. I wrote out a long telegram to Milo Perkins, then in charge of surplus products, and got it off at once. Then I followed up the telegram by a letter. In a few days a carload of surplus foods went to the local office of the Tennessee Department of Public Welfare with the request that the food be dispensed to the striking miners.

The CIO lost that strike, but I have heard that the men finally succeeded in organizing with the AF of L. I hope that they found some relief from their distressing situation.

That second night at Ducktown, Anderson took me around with him checking on the pickets at the various entrances of the mines. As we were about to set out he ran back and got his pistol, which he put in the car pocket saying, "I'd better have that because some-body might want to get me."

We drove out to the Hiawassee Dam which lay between two high promontories with the valley betwen them, drained of its river. Floodlights shone glaringly on the great natural cut between the banks, and steam shovels carried on their noisy and efficient job. It was a titanic, amazing scene. Whenever I have seen that particular dam since then, I still see its beginning.

That dam and its significance to the life of that area consoled me after my Ducktown visit, for it meant to me the use of land, water, and power in the service of people, as contrasted with the seared devastation of the Ducktown area.

WOODWORKERS INTERNATIONAL

Beginnings in Mississippi

In March, 1944, a CIO paper carried a story of the arrest and thirty-six-hour jailing of two representatives of the International Woodworkers of America, and the wife of one of them, in Jackson, Mississippi. No crime had been charged against any of them—that is, no crime except belonging to a CIO union. This seemed to warrant a trip to Jackson.

The city was crowded because of government workers, new industries, and the other activities stimulated in time of war. Not being able to get a hotel room I turned to the Young Women's Christian Association and got a room in its building. The general secretary, Miss Jean MacGillivray, remembered me from YWCA days and welcomed me with open arms.

Next morning my first visit was to the Right Reverend Duncan Gray, Bishop of Mississippi. We found we had many friends in common and I was impressed by his open-minded outlook and friendliness. When I left him to call on the chief of police, he said he would be glad to have me use his name as a reference. I asked him if he would look for me in the jail if I disappeared—he promised he would.

I went directly to the police chief's office, and had a cordial welcome. After a few minutes' talk about the city, I told him that my errand was to protect the civil rights of union people. He was not a tall man, but well built and with a military air. He rose to his feet, flushed, and said that if that was what I wanted to talk about I might as well leave. I said I was sorry, but I could not go until I had some assurance that a similar denial of civil rights would not happen again.

The chief said angrily, "Why is everybody talking to me about civil rights, civil rights, when all I am doing is to protect our war plants? I think more of my country than of what CIO people call civil rights involving only two or three people."

I asked him if the CIO people he had arrested carried any sort of weapons, and what they had done that was wrong. The chief replied, "First place, they didn't have any identification." I handed him my own CIO card and said the men must have carried something like that. He replied, "Those men didn't carry any kind of cards, and if they had I wouldn't know if they had forged them." Actually the police who arrested the men had taken their identification cards from them.

Handing him my air-travel aluminum credit card, I asked, "Do you think I could forge that?"

"You could, for all I know," he answered.

Again I asked him what the men had done that was wrong and dangerous. He replied, "These CIO men came in like snakes, they hung around our defense plants, slipping and sliding around in the dark on company property. They might have blown the plants up for all I knew. If you go slipping and sliding around these plants at night I'll put you in jail too."

I assured him I was not an organizer and would not be found "slipping around." As a matter of fact, the CIO men had not been to a defense plant. They were arrested in a business district in broad daylight.

In the course of our talk the chief said that he had been a union man, in one of the railroad brotherhoods. Thereupon I put this question to him, "I have come here to protect union representatives who are acting under constitutional and legal rights, and in accordance with the National Labor Relations Act. I am not going to leave this office until you tell me what you consider is the proper thing for these union men to do, before they begin to see workers."

As he began to speak I took out notebook and pencil and made notes. That excited him and he said, "You are just taking down what I say to take it to the FBI, and I won't say anything unless you put up that pencil."

"That is a good idea of yours," I said, "only I will take my charges to the Department of Justice, since they ask the FBI to make investigations." I waited until he decided to answer my question—and this was his pattern for organizing:

"First thing, I would require of a union man would be for him to go to the Chamber of Commerce and get its approval. He should also see the managers of the companies and ask them if they objected to his organizing their employees. The union should get an office, out in the open, on the main street where business people have their offices, so everybody could see what they were doing. The union men should get a permit from me."

I laughed heartily and said, "Chief, are you just being funny?" Is that the way your railroad union got organized?"

That time, when he stood up I stood up too. I departed with a suggestion that he obey the laws he was sworn to protect, and a reminder that he was committing offenses against fundamental rights of American citizens. I added my charges against the chief to those which the union officers had made and in due time someone representing the Department of Justice called on him. Thereafter the unions had no more interference from him.

The chief and I met a little more than a year later—again I called on him in his office, but this time he shook hands cordially and said he was glad to see me. We did not mention any painful subjects— we did talk about the rapid growth of a number of CIO unions in the city, and what good citizens these union men and women made.

After calling upon a number of responsible Jackson citizens and asking their help in making life and liberty safe for union folk, I made my last visit to the sheriff, who I heard was "all right on unions." He was just leaving his office when I met him so I merely stated my mission in Jackson and added that I had heard he understood about unions and they had no quarrel with him. He said little, which I believed was due to his haste. That was Saturday afternoon.

Sunday morning, Bishop Gray called for me at the YWCA in his automobile and we drove to Vicksburg, where he was to preach and I to spend a few days on my work.

Monday morning, Miss MacGillivray had a call from the sheriff. His wife was a member of the YWCA board of directors and there were cordial good feelings between them. The sheriff opened the conversation by asking, "Is a woman named Mason staying here?"

"No," was the answer, "but she was here for a few days last week."

Said the sheriff, "Did you know she was a subversive character?"

Again Miss MacGillivray answered no, and added that she had known Miss Mason in the YWCA for many years, and that she was well thought of in the Association.

Still seeking his clue, the sheriff said, "Did you know Miss Mason was working for a subversive and communistic organization?"

"No," said Miss MacGillivray, "but I know she is with the CIO."

"Do you know where she went when she left here?" inquired the sheriff.

"All I know is that she left here with Bishop Duncan Gray in his car Sunday morning." The baffled sheriff gave up hope of discovering a dangerous character in the shape of an elderly white-haired woman and I have not heard of him since.

Bishop Gray deposited me at my hotel that Sunday morning. I had enjoyed the drive, his companionship, and the sermon he preached.

In April, 1944, William Botkins, vice-president of the International Woodworkers, CIO, had written to George Brown, director of organization for the union, telling him of a situation in Vicksburg involving interference with civil rights. As this letter was one of the reasons for my visit to Vicksburg at this time, I quote from it:

We were returning to Vicksburg from a meeting at about 2:45 P.M., Sunday. . . . As we approached the entrance of the Union Hall we noticed three Vicksburg policemen standing in front of the hall. When we started to enter we were stopped by these policemen who asked who we were, and what we were doing in Vicksburg. We told them our names (Brother Bentley, Hawkins, and myself) and our business. Again we started to enter the hall and they told us that they were picking us up.

Youman, the local union president, was standing out in front and as we started to get into the prowler car, one of the police asked him who he was and said he had better come along too. They loaded the four of us into the car and took us to the police station. We were all . . . placed in separate rooms.

Then we were questioned by the police captain, lieutenant, and sergeant. I asked if we were under arrest, and if so, on what charge. I was told by the captain that we were not under arrest, but were being held for investigation. After I had been there for about half an hour the police captain came in to ask me a number of questions. . . . He wanted to know my full name and address, not my Memphis address, but the address I had on the West Coast. He wanted to know what position I held in the International Union, and what business I had in Vicksburg.

He questioned me as to why I was not in the armed services, and informed me that he had two sons who were in the service and that I looked to be a big, husky young man and I should be fighting for my country. I showed him my draft classification card and told him I was ready to serve any time I was called, and further that I had attempted to enlist in every branch of the service right after Pearl Harbor, but had been rejected because of poor eyesight. He inferred I was lying.

He then began to lecture, telling me that I was a stranger in the South, and that I knew nothing of the customs of the southern people—particularly the Negro race; that I was inciting trouble for the police department, and he guessed he would have to shoot up a bunch of "these burr-headed Negroes." *He told me that regardless of what federal laws might be passed, if the Negroes got out of place they would probably be lynched and the police department would not interfere.* [Italics mine.] I asked him what evidence he had that I, or any of the other union representatives, was causing this alleged trouble among the Negroes. He stated that he had had complaints from local citizens in Vicksburg. . . .

He advised me that if I was interested in winning the war I should catch the next train to the West Coast and stay there. . . . I was left alone for about an hour. Then they came and got me and took me into another room where I was questioned by the lieutenant. I was then returned to the courtroom where I stayed until about 5:30 P.M.

Some questions were asked the other three which were not asked of me—also different statements were made to each of us. The lieutenant informed Brother Bentley that we had been picked up for investigation at the request of the FBI. However, this statement was not made to any of the others.

In Vicksburg I had the good luck to find that Colonel Alexander Fitz Hugh, the city's leading citizen, and I were relatives. We were cousins on some five or six Virginia lines. His wife had attended my uncle's school for girls (Gunston Hall in Washington) and my first cousin, another Lucy Mason, was Mrs. Fitz Hugh's closest friend in her school days.

Colonel Fitz Hugh listened to my story with courtesy. He said that if the union came to his plant he would not oppose it, but he hoped his employees would decide against organizing. When we parted, the Colonel told me the names of a number of men that I might well see. He said that he would be glad to have me use his name for my reference, and that he had lived in Vicksburg a long time.

Colonel Fitz Hugh's name was a golden wand—I used it in all of my contacts and the only person I can recall who gave no response to it was the chief of police. But he was deaf, and in his anger because of a CIO representative's call he may not have heard me. I have never been in a city where one man's name more completely stood out for association with what was good and desirable than that of this gentleman, Colonel Fitz Hugh.

Notwithstanding the bold and threatening language of the "officers of the law" there was soon a marked decrease of lawlessness and violence on their part in Vicksburg. One of the things that helped was a visit by the district attorney to the chief of police, the news of which spread abroad. Another asset was the opportunity I had had to talk at length to my distant but manifold cousin, Colonel Fitz Hugh. This courteous gentlemen respected persons. His attitude toward me must have surprised the townspeople and undoubtedly had its results.

The most interesting event in that visit to Vicksburg was a meeting with three hundred or more woodworkers in a Negro church filled to overflowing. The pastor of the church took an active part in the meeting. He led in prayer and now and then burst into spontaneous petitions for blessings on the CIO which had come to give working people a better life. A union member led in singing hymns and Negro melodies. Several times I was referred to as "this white lady from heaven, who is here to help us." Once I was called "an angel," titles I had never been given before.

I was told that the local union had 600 union members, only five or six of whom were white. At first the local had voted two of the top offices to white members. But in a short time the Negroes told the white men that they were too few in number and too lacking in leadership to hold the top offices. They asked that Negroes be elected. This was done and I was told that the Negroes made good officers.

While I was still in Vicksburg, one of the CIO men suggested that I drive with him to Port Gibson to meet with a good group of women crate-and-basket workers who had been building a union for a year or two. The National Labor Relations Board had ordered the company to cease and desist from certain unfair labor practices, and the Court had upheld the Board's decision. The workers were looking forward to a Labor Board election, as the majority had joined the union.

Port Gibson is a little distance back from the river bank. Our meeting that night was held in a Negro Methodist Church. The pastor welcomed us and opened and closed the meeting with prayer. As usual, I made a union talk. The response was enthusiastic.

Since the company stubbornly refused to negotiate with the union, the workers came out on strike, some time later.

Months after this trip I had a long distance telephone call from George Bentley, representative of the United Woodworkers, saying that the sheriff was waving his gun at the picket line at Port Gibson and threatening to shoot the women full of lead unless they went back to work. I pointed out that I could not get there by any means of travel in time to relieve the danger he reported. So I used telephone, telegrams, and air mail special delivery letters.

First, I got Bentley to tell me just what had happened. Then I dictated a telegram from him to send to the chief of the Civil Rights

Section, Department of Justice, stating his charges against the sheriff and requesting an immediate investigation. Then I telephoned to the Civil Rights Section asking quick action. I was instructed to put my charges in writing and hasten them. Then I wired Sheriff M. M. Montgomery at Port Gibson, repeating the telegram I had sent the Department of Justice, and adding the following telegram:

Just received information regarding your use of threats to shoot striking workers on picket line at woodworking plant in Port Gibson. You are obviously violating Federal laws protecting rights of workers to organize and to picket when on strike. Am appealing to U. S. Department of Justice for investigation of your acts.

Next morning I received a telegram from the Department of Justice, which read as follows:

Telegram on Port Gibson Mississippi received and will have attention.

Just to be on the safe side I wired duplicates of that telegram to Sheriff Montgomery and George Bentley.

Silence settled over Port Gibson so far as I was concerned. However, I was reasonably sure the Department of Justice with its usual efficiency in such matters had begun proceedings to make the union women's lives secure. Mr. Bentley sent an excellent statement to the Department, substantiating my communications.

In about ten days came a letter from Bentley, written in his Memphis office, assuring me that "something has completely changed the attitude of the Port Gibson officials and the citizens as a whole. However, the sheriff has disappeared from Port Gibson and the report was made to me that three men in a car came into Port Gibson on Tuesday, May 14, and took him away."

Much later I met Turner Smith, chief of the Civil Rights Section at that time, and asked him what had happened in the Port Gibson case, and how he had succeeded in relieving danger in the situation in such short time. He replied that since my telegram and telephone call had indicated that there might be bloodshed unless something was done at once, he had asked the Department of Justice to get the FBI from Jackson into Port Gibson as quickly as possible.

The mere appearance of the FBI men had been enough to convince the law-breaking local officers of the law that they had better mend their ways.

Such stories as these about the United Wooodworkers in Mississippi show the hostile reception they received when first organizing in that state. But there was a Mississippian who saw things differently and told a newspaper man about it. I had the good luck to pick up the story.

Hodding Carter, publisher and editor of the *Delta Democrat Times,* Greenville, Miss., is a distinguished southerner who keeps his eyes open, travels a great deal, and sees more than most people.

Mr. Carter had said that he wanted to see unions grow in the South because they had a beneficial effect on the economy. I quote some interesting bits from the reporter's interview:

"As a publisher," Mr. Carter said, "I have to keep informed on advertising expenditures and other business barometers, particularly in cities in my region of size comparable with my own town of Greenville—which has a population of about 35,000."

Mr. Carter said he had especially watched Laurel, Mississippi, also in the 35,000 class, which a few years ago did not have labor organizations, but which today had 6500 CIO members.

"CIO union contracts have added more than five million dollars to Laurel's annual payrolls," he said. "There is much more business activity in Laurel than in other cities of the same size in my area. And particularly I know there is more newspaper advertising carried in the local paper in Laurel than in these other cities."

Mr. Carter was speaking in 1946. The figures would be larger now, for still more union contracts have since been secured by the CIO in Laurel.

Looking back at the struggles of the woodworkers in Mississippi six or more years ago, I realize that each set of workers has had to fight the same battles and face almost the same lawless treatment by "the law." But the people are persistent and go ahead building their unions in spite of obstacles. Three or four years ago I spent some time in several towns south of Atlanta where a similar battle was enacted before determined workers finally won union-management agreements and conditions improved.

Southern director for the International Woodworkers is now Emil Luter, in his early days an automobile union member. Born in Randolph County, Arkansas, his is unmistabably southern, a man of strong physique and determination, and a hard worker.

The man who now carries the over-all burden of organizing in a "tough state" for organizers is Robert W. Starnes, CIO director for both Mississippi and Louisiana. Mr. Starnes is a native of Mississippi and has spent most of his life there. He is a tall, well built man with pleasant manners, and your first glance might classify him as a professional man. When the Communications Workers of America, CIO, was in process of organization in Mississippi, Bob Starnes was one of the southern leaders, and he remained in the telephone industry for some time.

Judging by several communications I have received from Mr. Starnes in recent months, there has been real progress by CIO unions since I was in Mississippi. He mentions casually that all of the building-board plants in the state are organized, including the big Masonite plant at Laurel. Woodworking leads in organization, and he reports many plants organized in Laurel, Hattiesburg, Jackson, and Natchez.

The Piney Woods

The organizing wave among the woodworkers of the southern states came chiefly from beyond the Mississippi River and swept through Mississippi, Louisiana, and Arkansas into Tennessee, Alabama, Georgia, and other states.

In all of the South there was opposition to the union, an opposition made more intense because the majority of the workers involved were Negroes. To the employers this was interference with their own special prerogative of "cheap labor."

In the summer of 1947 the CIO, responding to requests for help in organizing, sent representatives into the town of Cuthbert, Georgia, some two hundred miles south of Atlanta, where there were several woodworking plants. The employees were chiefly Negroes but the white men were also desirous of building a union.

W. M. Rowe and J. R. Cochran of Atlanta, members of the CIO staff, were in charge of organizing. Messrs. Rowe and Cochran had been on the job for five or six weeks before opposition to the union became evident. Mr. Rowe's report on Cuthbert includes the following:

> The Negroes want the union very much and about 95 per cent of them are signed up as members. Half of the white men are also signed up. There are about 500 working in the three plants in Cuthbert.
>
> Our meetings have been held in three Negro churches. . . . We have also met in the Mutual Aid Band Hall.

Mr. Cochran, in an affidavit for the Department of Justice charging denial of civil rights, said in part:

> Last night at a meeting we held in Payne Chapel, two carloads of white people drove up to the church about ten minutes to nine and sat in their cars till nine o'clock when the meeting started. Mr. Harris, a merchant, and several other white men left the cars and stood around the doors and windows of the church. Among them were the sheriff, the county clerk, and the solicitor.
>
> When Mr. Rowe began to speak I went outside the church for a smoke and saw two policemen standing at a window listening.

Mr. Cochran said that he had explained the civil rights of working men who wanted to join a union, and soon after that the white men who had been in the church withdrew.

The meeting adjourned about 10:20, and Messrs. Rowe and Cochran returned to the hotel. Cochran said that he could see a crowd of twenty to thirty men which had formed in the city square directly opposite the room in which he and Rowe were watching. He said that carloads of men continually drove around the square, while other men on foot milled around. The police seemed to be fraternizing with the mob and not trying to disperse it.

This was the night of July 31, 1947. The morning of August 1, Douglas Brittenham, hotel manager, told the CIO men what had happened inside the hotel while they were watching the crowd from their window.

Mr. Brittenham said that the night clerk called him when the crowd collected and a man named Sealy demanded the keys of the CIO men's rooms. The clerk refused Sealy's demand and called Mr. Brittenham. Mr. Brittenham then called the mayor, the chief of police, and the sheriff requesting that they all come at once to the hotel, that he stood on his civil rights and no one could invade his home without legal warrant. He said he looked to the officers to protect those rights. All three of the men called upon arrived quickly and dispersed the crowd. Sealy, who had a gun concealed in his shirt, disappeared when the officials came.

It must have been a dramatic moment when Douglas Brittenham stood with outstretched arms at the bottom of the lobby stairs and announced that he was standing on his federally guaranteed civil rights. More men of his type are needed. Mr. Cochran quoted Mr. Brittenham as saying that he did not care whether we worked for the CIO or AF of L, or whoever we were with; that our characters were irreproachable and any time we wanted a room he would have it for us. (I occupied a room in his hotel shortly after this.)

Cuthbert's business men and city officials next turned to the passage of an ordinance requiring that any one soliciting members for unions should first secure a city license and pay "a license fee of $1500 a year for organizing labor."

Charlie Gillman was the first to test this ordinance. A union meeting was called to which he spoke and invited membership in the CIO. He was promptly arrested and had some difficulty getting bond at a preliminary trial, as the local agent, a banker, was doing all in his power to harass union people. A long trip was necessary to secure bond and keep Mr. Gillman out of "the stockade" to which he was sentenced.

After a second trial some days later, in which CIO attorney Jerome Cooper pointed out the unconstitutionality of such an ordinance, Gillman was found guilty and bond was again made. Since everyone involved knew that the U. S. Supreme Court, and several courts in Georgia, had held that such ordinances were null and void because of their deprivation of the civil right of free speech, that was the end of the matter.

John Ramsay and I were present at the trial and when it was over
he introduced me to the mayor who had acted as judge. I said to the
mayor-judge,

"Mr. Mayor, today you have broken and defied the Bill of Rights."

Questioned the mayor, "What is the Bill of Rights?"

I replied, "It is part of the U. S. Constitution guaranteeing civil
rights of free speech, free assembly, and other freedoms."

To this the mayor replied, "We don't need any of that in
Cuthbert."

While I was in Cuthbert, several interesting days were spent calling on city officials—sheriff, police, mayor, the banker who had
made it hard to get Gillman's first bond, the editor, some of the
ministers and business men. The banker was pleasant to talk with
and confessed he knew nothing about unions. Some of the ministers
were fine.

Sheriff and chief of police were reminded that they were denying
Negro workers their civil rights when they tried to intimidate them
and keep them out of the union. These officers thought that the less
civil rights some people had the better.

The mayor and I pursued the subject of civil rights further in a
talk in his office. When I tried to explain to him the meaning of civil
rights applied to meetings, to the use of public thoroughfares, and
to speech, the mayor said, "We never heard of anything like that
down here—the only laws we know are the local laws."

In some years, however, the picture in Cuthbert was to brighten.
The woodworking plants in Cuthbert today are under collective bargaining agreements, with only one exception. While under separate
contracts with their companies, the unions have one joint local for
all members of the International Woodworkers of America, CIO.
Bruce Bloodworth, who is now on the Woodworkers staff in this
region, reports that a union agreement which has been in existence
for two years has recently been renewed. There has been a vast improvement for the organized woodworkers in Cuthbert, and the
members appreciate the good things gained for them by collective
bargaining. "In union there is strength" remains true.

How Not to Lose an Election

The man who has worked out a successful formula on "How not to lose a Labor Board Election" is W. Rubert Thrasher, a representative of the CIO Organizing Committee. In the six years he has been on the CIO staff Mr. Thrasher has lost only one election—and in that he did not follow the formula. He is a quiet, dignified looking man with pleasant manners, who inspires confidence quickly.

Mr. Thrasher and I first met soon after he had helped organize several hundred employees in a shoe and leather plant located in a town not far from Atlanta. He had the advantage of organizing on the inside early in the campaign since he was an employee of the company, and his fellow workers elected him president of their union. The membership increased rapidly and the great majority were soon signed up. H. W. Denton of the CIO staff helped from the beginning.

The union leaders soon decided an open meeting would solidify the people. The only place in town big enough to hold such a meeting was the high school and that was readily secured, for many of the union members, like Mr. Thrasher, were solid and respected citizens. Charlie Gillman and I were asked to speak at this meeting and we drove out together.

As we approached the high school we were met by a large crowd coming away from the school. Our hearts sank, for we thought they were breaking up the meeting. Coming closer we realized that one set of people were pouring into the building while others were coming out. Mr. Thrasher and the others in charge, realizing that there would be an overflow gathering, had arranged for a meeting at 6 o'clock and another at 7. The place was packed, all seats taken, some people leaning against the wall and others sitting in the open windows and standing in the doors. The speakers had an ovation and the meeting was a great success.

Shortly thereafter union strength was shown in a large majority vote when the Labor Board election was held. Mrs. Thrasher was so helpful in this organizing campaign that when she gave up the office job she had with the company, the union elected her secretary. Later on she came on the CIO staff as one of the office secretaries. Mr. Thrasher was put on the staff of the CIO Organizing Committee in May, 1946, working chiefly in the Atlanta area. Having heard Mr. Thrasher discuss his formula for not losing elections, I asked him to describe it to me for inclusion in this book—for knowing how not to lose elections is as important as knowing how to win them. I quote Mr. Thrasher:

"I learned the formula at a Shoeworkers convention in Worcester, Massachusetts, around 1943. (I was with the Shoeworkers union for some years before coming on the CIO staff.) At that time Walter Harris of the CIO staff had been loaned to the Shoeworkers. He was giving a lot of reports on elections that had been won in other parts of the shoe industry. He said that the yardstick he used was to discount all of the 'live' cards he had by twenty per cent and make sure that sixty per cent of the workers in a plant were signed up, *after* discounting the twenty per cent. Then you were sure to win. Harris said he had lost only one election in the time covered, which was about four years—and he did not go by the yardstick in the election he had lost.

"Since then I have always tried as nearly as possible to go by that yardstick and I have lost one election out of thirty in six years. Believe it or not, I slipped up in that election by not living up to the formula; the committee had insisted on going ahead with the election regardless of whether or not they had a proper number of signed cards."

Mr. Thrasher then gave the rest of his win-elections formula:

"In addition, you must have a good, strong committee in the plant. No organizer organizes a plant himself—the committee of workers must do the organizing—all organizers can do is to advise and assist the committee. The organizer must build this committee around himself. The committee must like the organizer and follow his leadership. In other words the organizer, so far as the committee is concerned, is the most important man in the CIO, because the plant workers do not know President Philip Murray, or Vice-President Allan Haywood, or the other high officers.

"One other thought: an organizer must never try to be a big shot. Just be yourself. This is the only way I know to organize."

TELEPHONES AND YOUTH

The young and vigorous telephone workers, organized in the South within the past ten years, have taken their place in CIO since World War II. How that came about is one of the stories which deserves a place in this book, although it is not a part of my own story.

The Communications Workers of America is a true industrial union, with more than 32,000 members in the Southern District. W. A. Smallwood is district director; G. E. Gill, assistant director. Bill Smallwood is still in his early forties after nearly ten years of active and responsible leadership. Comparative youthfulness would seem to be a characteristic of most telephone union leaders. The able and respected Joe Beirne, international president with headquarters in Washington, is in the same age bracket. And this youthfulness is apparent as well in the membership as a whole—one of the major segments of the union is made up of "bobby-soxers"! But more of that in a moment.

Smallwood was born on a South Georgia farm, where his family raised tobacco. After two years at Antioch College, where he majored in Business Administration, he returned to the family farm, and from there went into the telephone company. He was a central office repairman when he was called into full-time union activity.

He tells the story of CWA in the South in his own words.

"CWA is very much of the present, and the Southern district is even more so. But if our history is short, we can't complain about a lack of excitement. It's been rugged all the way; and like the telephone man who climbs the poles, we've had our ups and downs.

"The challenge we faced was doubled by the fact that, as we began to organize ourselves into our first real union, the telephone company had already reached industrial maturity.

"We knew what we wanted, but we were almost entirely on our own. If a group ever pulled itself up by its bootstraps, it was ours. Sacrifices that had been made by men and women in other industries were an inspiration to us, yet the fact that we were organizing an employee group composed mainly of the "white collar" class meant that we were charting our own maps as we went along.

"Add to that the nature of the industry itself—the telephone being a public utility—and you have an idea of the background.

"For generations, the massive Bell System (which accounts for 85 per cent of all telephone business) had prevented a genuine labor movement within its employee body. The spirit was always there. Telephone strikes were recorded in the 1890's, the early 1900's, and a strike of telephone workers in Atlanta, Georgia, toward the close of World War I brought the plight of these employees to the attention of the nation.

"The spirit was there, but the company fought it to the last ditch. You are familiar with the impressive advertising which the company places in magazines and newspapers, selling the idea that telephone workers are 'different.' This has been going on for many years.

"At the same time, the company was putting forth an equal effort to convince their empolyees that they really were different. Nobody in the Bell system had a job—everybody had a 'position.' We were all just a little bit better than people who *worked* for a living.

"Sounds incredible? You should have been there. It was a masterful job, and almost succeeded in its objective. Along with this, the company provided its employees with 'associations' and thoughtfully saw to it that 'dues' were five cents per month. In addition, the company graciously allowed its employees to meet in rent-free halls. In short, the industry worked with one hand to taint the idea of 'unionism,' and on the other hand, sopped up union-spirit in its illegal 'associations.'

"So it was that 'The Voice With a Smile' became a national symbol of the satisfied employee. How did it happen that this same attractive young woman, together with the thousands of skilled craftsmen, installers, repairmen, clerks, and others organized and established, in less than ten years, one of the most militant and progressive unions in the CIO?

"It didn't happen all at once but when the Fifth District Federal Court put Southern Bell's illegal 'association' out of business in 1942, the snowball was started on its way.

"Suppressed unionism blossomed spontaneously in scores of towns throughout the South. In nine states, from Alabama, Florida, Georgia, Kentucky, Louisiana, Mississippi, North Carolina, South Carolina, and Tennessee, groups of workers got together and spread the word along the grapevine over the whole territory covered by Southern Bell.

"Perhaps it was because the company's headquarters were in Atlanta that organizing activity focused there. At any rate, we soon had the campaign going as well as it could without funds and with so little outside assistance. We worked at nights and on weekends, cranking out handbills on a hand-operated mimeograph, and coordinating the efforts of our fellow workers in the nine states.

"The National Federation of Telephone Workers, a loosely organized body of independent unions in other parts of the country, sent all the help it could spare. One of our first objectives was to organize ourselves into the Southern Federation of Telephone Workers and to join hands with NFTW in an effort to make ourselves heard in the giant Bell system.

"We found we had to do it the hard way. Bitterly resentful of the organizational activity, the company fired broadside after broadside at us, on every front.

"In addition to the usual methods, the telephone company had at its disposal a significantly large supervisory force. As the union made headway, the company continued to increase its supervisors until that force reached enormous size. Supervisors were instructed by the company to do actual production work outside the range of management functions. Today there are enough supervisors on the industry's payroll to account for one out of every four or five of its total employees.

"These supervisors were used in two ways; first, to carry out a policy of paternalism—or maternalism, as we call it in the Bell system, in line with our habit of referring to 'Ma' Bell—on a gigantic scale, and second, to provide the threat of a handy strike-breaking force.

"They tried everything—but membership climbed, and we won recognition. Each time we changed our union structure, to make the union stronger, we were faced with a move on the part of the company to challenge our right to represent the workers, and each time we won out. Much more than in other unions, we have had to retain legal counsel in order to outwit the legalistic blockades set up in our path by the Bell companies.

"One other threat which hung over the employees of the telephone company relates to the nature of the industry itself.

"A skilled telephone worker must work for the telephone company, or start over somewhere else at the bottom. A truck driver, for instance, can quit one company and go to work driving a truck somewhere else. It isn't that way in our business. The skills utilized by the telephone industry become uniquely telephonic. Switchboard operators, installers, repairmen, central office craftsmen, and many others would not be in a position to obtain comparable employment with any other industry. Even the accounting methods of the company are such that an accountant who had become versed in these methods would find it difficult to utilize that skill elsewhere.

"That situation works to the company's advantage in rate cases, as well as in labor relations, but I cite it only as an indication of the enormous pressure that the System can exert on its employees to be good little boys and girls.

"The time came when every member was put to the acid test. Recognition had brought us to the bargaining table, where improvements were won in our working conditions. But it soon became evident that we would never settle the question of wages at the table.

"In 1947, the year in which we officially became the Communications Workers, the time had come to show our economic strength for the first time. It was an interesting moment. These telephone workers had never hit the bricks. They hardly knew what the term meant.

They had been educated to deplore strikes. They had been told that they were not like other workers. And they knew that they didn't have a dime in their treasury. But—they walked out.

"For six weeks they stayed out, in spite of the fact that they had nothing to start with except their faith. At crucial moments, when the outlook was blackest, morale and material support was forthcoming from the outside. Outright grants were given by the larger unions in CIO, and a substantial loan was made by the United Mine Workers. Still, looked at in the cold light of reasoning, it was impossible. But the warm spirit of faith and mutual assistance made it possible.

"When the strike ended, the company knew it had a union on its hands.

"We had our own wounds to lick. Most of all, we needed a strong national union, and we needed to become a part of the overall labor movement. At our next convention, we in the Southern district began to plug for affiliation with CIO. It took two years, but the motion went through in a burst of enthusiasm at our convention in 1949. We wanted to become a part of CIO for two sound reasons:

"First, telephone workers needed to be organized on industry lines, rather than as craft groups;

"Second, the aims and ideals of the CIO were progressive and forward-looking, in line with our own ideals.

"Speaking for the membership in the South, I think we owe a particular debt to CIO. In the earlier days of organizing, in steel, textiles, rubber, and other industries below the Mason-Dixon line, broken heads were suffered and blood was shed by devoted people who were attempting to organize underpaid Southern workers.

"We feel that those sacrifices helped to make our own progress more rapid. So we are happy to think that telephone workers in more than six hundred communities in the South can repay their debt in carrying to all corners of the region the benefits of unionism."

Recently, while visiting CWA's offices in Atlanta, I talked with Sam Sims, a staff representative who has been active in the union since its inception, and who still looks, after years of organizing and bargaining in the trade union movement, like a benevolent banker. I wanted to know more about those "bobby-soxers."

I asked him, "Do they make good union members?"

"Not only that—they make up the heart of the union," Sims told me. "Women, many of them still in their teens, account for sixty-five per cent of our membership. They enter into union work in a wonderful way, and when it's necessary to carry a picket sign, they're enthusiastic about that, too."

Bobby-soxers on the picket line! The South has changed, hasn't it?

Chapter IV

THE LAW

Civil Rights

WITH A life-long interest in the rights of people and the defense of those rights, when I found myself working for new labor unions, in the deep South, I drew heavily on federal guarantees of such rights. In my travels I found it useful to carry with me a typewritten list of those guarantees embedded in federal law. Eventually, this typewritten list gave way to a blue and red pamphlet, entitled *Your Civil Rights,* and prepared by the legal department of the CIO at the suggestion of Van A. Bittner. This pamphlet contains quotations from the Bill of Rights and the subsequent laws and supreme court decisions which related most closely to union operations.

Heading the list are the guarantees of civil rights afforded by the constitution through the Amendments in the Bill of Rights. The First Amendment states that

Congress shall make no law respecting an establishment of religion, or prohibiting the free exercise thereof; or abridging the freedom of speech, or of the press; or the right of the people peaceably to assemble, and to petition the Government for a redress of grievances.

The Fourteenth Amendment extends the prohibitions contained in earlier amendments specifically to the states, saying, in part,

No State shall make or enforce any law which shall abridge the privileges or immunities of citizens of the United States; nor shall any

93

State deprive any person of life, liberty or property, without due process of law; nor deny to any person within its jurisdiction the equal protection of the laws.

Mob violence is enjoined in the Criminal Code, which provides that

if two or more persons conspire to injure, oppress, threaten, or intimidate any citizen in the free exercise or enjoyment of any right or privilege secured to him by the Constitution or laws of the United States, or because of his having so exercised the same . . . they shall be fined not more than $5,000.00 and imprisoned not more than ten years. . . ."

During its brief existence between June 1933 and May 1935, the National Recovery Act (NRA) provided, in its famous Section 7A, an effective stimulus to union organization. That section stated, in part, that

employees shall have the right to organize and bargain collectively through representatives of their own choosing, and shall be free from the interference, restraint, or coercion of employers of labor, or of their agents, in the designation of such representatives or in self-organization or in other concerted activities for the purpose of collective bargaining or other mutual aid or protection.

Two months after the NRA came to an end, the National Labor Relations Act, known as the Wagner Act, came into being, and was subsequently upheld by the Supreme Court. This act spells out the right of employees

to self-organization, to form, join, or assist labor organizations, to bargain collectively through representatives of their own choosing, and to engage in concerted activities, for the purpose of collective bargaining or other mutual aid or protection.

Thus labors gains from the NRA continued to be the law of the land.

It has remained for the Supreme Court to interpret these constitutional and statutory provisions in specific terms. In a series of important decisions, the highest court of the United States has affirmed the right of labor to distribute union literature, to solicit members, to call and hold labor meetings, and to picket peacefully.

It has, furthermore, reasserted that these rights cannot be infringed by employer, state, or municipality.

In its conclusion, *Your Civil Rights* points out that

even where the Constitution clearly forbids certain conduct and even where the Supreme Court has said it forbids certain conduct, the people must be vigilant to make sure that their rights are kept alive. A right is somthing like a muscle in the human body. If you don't use it, if you don't exercise it, it becomes weak and powerless.

Many are the ways in which I have used the blue and red pamphlet to educate local officers. In some instances, when I come to a town before any trouble has occurred, I innocently take out my list and say,

"I am so glad that the officers of the law in Jonesville know the federal laws under which they are operating. I won't have to make any charges to the Department of Justice from this town and county!"

After that, there is rarely any breach of rights in that place. Ordinarily, an officer denying someone his civil rights abandons the unlawful procedure as soon as he is informed of the nature of his act. At times it is useful to hint that the federal government will be notified of any further breaches. But if these measures fail, it is always possible to appeal to the Civil Rights Section of the Department of Justice, and, finally, to the courts of law.

I am often asked about my procedure in making charges to the Department of Justice against officers of the law who have themselves violated such federally guaranteed civil rights as free speech, free assembly, and free access to streets and public highways.

In making these charges I am always careful to show just what has been done to deny such rights. For instance, when an officer stops the distribution of union literature, he has denied the right of free speech guaranteed in the Bill of Rights—for the printed word is as important as the spoken word in spreading information. These federally guaranteed rights defined in detail in Supreme Court decisions, also include free assembly in a building or a park, and unhampered access to paths, roads, and streets commonly used by the public, including mill village streets and walk-ways connecting the entrance of a factory and the public street.

If the affidavits or statements we submit in substantiation of our charges indicate a civil rights denial, it is customary for the Civil Rights Section of the Department of Justice to ask either the district attorney or the FBI to make an investigation and submit a report.

There was an interesting example of this process in the town of Ellijay, Georgia, in the early summer of 1943. Frank Barker and others, of the Textile Workers Union, were working with textile employees in Ellijay who wanted help in forming a union. Both the sheriff and chief of police were pushing the union men around and ordering them to leave town.

Chief of Police Milton was father of the county sheriff, and the two formed a tight combination against union people.

Barker asked my help in presenting charges to the Department of Justice. I prepared them and presented supplemental evidence. As usual in such cases, copies of these papers were sent to Mr. M. Neil Andrews, then District Attorney of the Northern District of Georgia, a man of broad and unusual experience as an investigator and prosecutor for the federal government.

When Mr. Andrews had received all of our charges against the Ellijay police chief, he decided to try prevention rather than prosecution. Convinced that our complaints were well-founded, he suggested to the Attorney General that he, Mr. Andrews, should go to Ellijay and explain to the officers the civil rights provisions of the Constitution and laws of the United States. The Attorney General consented, and Mr. Andrews went to see the chief of police, Milton. He could not see the sheriff, since he was out of town.

Mr. Andrews explained to the police chief that "under the Free Speech and Press provisions of the Federal Constitution, it appeared that labor organizers had the right to do the things they were said to have been doing in Ellijay, unless and until they created a disorder and interfered with the passage of traffic through the streets and highways." The chief replied that for forty years they had been running anybody out of town they wanted to, and he guessed they would keep it up. Mr. Andrews reports, "About that time, the mayor, Mr. Holden, a rather young and progressive businessman, approached us, and when I explained the controversy to the mayor and stated my views of the rights of organizers, he said to the chief: 'Well, I agree with Mr. Andrews about the matter, and hereafter you must not interfere with people unless they violate the law relating to disorderly conduct and obstructing the streets.' "

Mr. Andrews said he complimented the mayor on his approach to the problem. Though the mill was not organized and the union men later on withdrew of their own accord, there were no further complaints of civil rights violations.

In many cases involving civil rights it is the ironical fact that "the law"—that is, the men appointed to uphold the law in the various localities—are the very men who break the law by denying workers their rights. Mayors, sheriffs, chiefs of police have been so busy protecting the rights of property and "keeping the peace" that they are quite ready to deny many other rights—such as those of free movement, speech, and assembly—when they see these as a possible threat to peace and property.

The chief of police at one city I visited was a retired army officer—deaf and opposed to labor unions. To prevent organization among industrial workers, the chief had several techniques. At first he had organizers arrested soon after they appeared in the city. He held them in jail as suspicious characters, later releasing them through the jail's back door, where a group of men forced them into an automobile, took them off in the woods, beat them, and ordered them never to come back.

This aroused such widespread newspaper blasts that the chief adopted a milder method of intimidation. When a union representative came to town to attend a meeting, he was arrested as soon as he got to the union hall and, along with some of the local union officers, taken to police headquarters and detained for two or three hours. When released, the representative would go back to the union meeting usually to find it dissolved, the frightened workers having gone home.

I was warned by friendly townspeople that I would not meet with a cordial reception from the chief. They were correct! Having a southern tradition of being polite to women (depending on who the women were), the chief of police rose to greet me, shook hands over the broad, high rail that separated him from the rest of the office, and said he was glad to see me. (Having white hair, what one newspaper man called a mild look, and a southern voice are advantages in first contacts in the South.)

When the chief learned my occupation, he quickly returned to his armchair behind the rail and indicated that the conversation was at an end. He was quite deaf, which gave him an advantage. Nevertheless, I shouted out to him that he had violated workers' civil rights and it would be my painful duty to see that a formal complaint was filed with the Department of Justice. At the end of each statement I made, he would roar in a huge voice, "You will!" or "That so?" or other two-word comments.

On the way out I met an intelligent looking officer and said to him, "Mr. Officer, you have the stupidest police chief I have ever met."

Said he, "Lady, you don't know half!"

In due time, the Department of Justice responded to the complaint filed by the union and me, and somehow got it through the chief's head that there were federal laws that must be observed even in his state.

A year after this visit I went back to see how things were. There had been an election and change of administration. The former police chief was retired. In his stead I found the intelligent officer who had agreed with my estimate of his former chief on the previous visit.

Gaffney, South Carolina

Not often does the local newspaper carry a headline such as the one carried by the *Spartanburg News* on March 6, 1940. "Investigation By U. S. At Gaffney Sought By Union," it read. The news story went on to say, "State officials of the Textile Workers Union of

America last night declared that they would appeal to the United States Department of Justice, and the Senate Civil Liberties Committee to launch an immediate investigation into what they termed lawlessness and terrorism directed against an organizational campaign among Gaffney textile workers."

The Hamrick Mills at Gaffney, South Carolina, were then the Alma, Limestone, and Hamrick Plants. (These mills have since changed ownership.) Their history of union-fighting goes back a long way. From 1936 to '38 the National Labor Relations Board has extensive reports from hearings on union charges of civil rights violations and unfair labor practices in Gaffney. Indeed, any organization making investigations into employer lawlessness in that period, or before or after it, would most likely find the three Hamrick Mills among the offenders.

Gaffney was always known as a "union-busting town." Before the CIO entered the picture, the Hamrick management had crushed a long strike against substandard wages and the stretch-out in their plants. This strike was noted for open violence against the workers. An overseer, for example, had used a shotgun to pump buckshot into the back of a picket as the unionist was returning home from picket duty. Another union leader was shot to death in broad daylight as he walked out of the company store. On another occasion the company imported guards from a private strike-breaking agency to drive pickets from the streets in front of one of their mills.

When the TWUA came into Gaffney, Dr. Witherspoon Dodge, a minister and a Textile Union representative, held a meeting in a public area before the Alma Mill. This meeting was forcibly broken up by anti-union thugs who stoned Dr. Dodge in the presence of law enforcement officers. But Dr. Dodge's calm courage in facing the mob and calling upon them to go back caused the mob to withdraw and prevented physical combat between the two groups.

Later on the management established a company union. When the leaders of the TWUA in the Limestone mill refused to join the company's "Red Apple Club," as it was called, both supervisory and anti-union workers met them one morning as they entered the plant door, blocked their passage, and would not permit them to go to work. Only the decisive action of the governor, who sent highway patrolmen to the plant immediately, broke up this type of mob action and saved the union leaders' jobs.

In 1939 and in the winter and spring of 1940, several rough incidents took place in Gaffney. Don McKee, TWUA staff member, was distributing leaflets before the Hamrick Mill gate when a man named Lee Dowdle attempted to grab them all. Don tried to retain his bundle of literature, whereupon Dowdle hit him on the head with a brick.

Don came in for more mob action when he went with, and in, the car of S. O. Neal, inspector for the Wage-Hour Division of the U. S. Department of Labor, to check on union claims that Hamrick employees were being defrauded of their full pay. A mob gathered about Neal's car, shouting and cursing and threatening the two men. After blocking the path of the automobile, the mob made efforts to overturn it, but Neal finally managed to drive away and escape. Among the words hurled at McKee and Neal, these are reported by witnesses—"To Hell with the federal government," "We don't give a damn about the federal government," "You ain't got no business here," "Let's tar and feather them."

As a result of further assaults like these, federal officials from other governmental departments called in by the union to investigate substandard conditions in the Hamrick Mills refused to enter Gaffney. Instead they conducted their inquiries from a town twenty miles away, interviewing witnesses driven back and forth by the union.

When William Spencer, field examiner for the National Labor Relations Board, came to look into the situation, however, he wanted to get an actual picture of conditions in Gaffney. Don accompanied Mr. Spencer to the Alma Mill village, driving in Spencer's car. Again the government man and the union man were threatened by a gang, but they managed to whip the car around and drive out without physical assault.

Dodging bullets and bricks became a grim necessity to Don Mc-

Kee, but he did not stop his activities in Gaffney on behalf of the workers who wanted organization. He is a good actor. I remember the union meeting at which he reported on his adventures around the Hamrick Mills. He acted as he talked and told what had happened the day following his assault at the Hamrick Mill gate, when he and two workers had returned to distribute handbills again at the change of shift. The police had promised to be present at the scene to prevent further attacks on the union people, but five minutes before the shift change, all the officers had disappeared leaving McKee and his party alone. As the workers came out of the mill, many of those opposed to the union openly carried small arms. In a moment bursting with tenseness, the armed men surrounded the three union members as Don and his friends continued passing out the leaflets. (A woman stopped a man from shooting Don from concealment behind a tree.)

During this period, many of the anti-union men carried pistols or shotguns. It was generally believed that an arsenal of at least twelve guns and a large box of ammunition was located in a department of the Alma Mill. Mr. Christopher told me that "sand bags in barricade style were then in plain view on top of the Alma plant." It was also reported that the company had a machine gun on top of the Alma Mill, behind the barricade.

Paul Christopher asked me to come into the situation, as a morale builder and speaker—but especially to help prepare affidavits to be sent to the Department of Justice and National Labor Relations Board in proof of the charges that were being made. I also got in personal touch with the Department of Justice, urging federal action. The justice of the union's claims was later revealed when the FBI conducted a full-scale investigation of civil liberty violations in Gaffney.

Some time later, the National Labor Relations Board upheld the union's claims and ordered the Hamrick management to reinstate in their jobs some twenty-three discharged union members and to pay them thousands of dollars in back wages. As a result of evidence presented by the TWUA, the Federal Wage and Hour Administration also found the company guilty of violating the minimum wage provisions of the Wage-Hour Act and scores of workers received back-pay checks for wages illegally withheld from them. Even the federal Walsh-Healey board, dealing with wages in government contracts, discovered the company in violation of wage and hour provisions and caused distribution of additional large sums of back pay to the workers.

One of the arguments often used by local authorities against the CIO was that the community could manage its own affairs if it were not for the outsiders who came in and made trouble. We were not surprised to hear this repeated at Gaffney. Yet the only "outsiders" who came in on this situation were government men, and Neal, the Wage-Hour inspector, came from a town only ten miles away.

As for the organizers, Paul Revere Christopher, in charge of the Hamrick organizing efforts, was born at Easley, S. C. At the time of this story Mr. Christopher was director of the Textile Workers Union in South Carolina.

Don McKee, the son of a minister, was a North Carolinian who came on the TWUA staff soon after he graduated from the University of North Carolina. By profession a teacher, he saw action in Europe in World War II with a mortar battalion, and returned to the organizing staff of the Textile Workers Union, after the war.

COLUMBIA, S. C., TRIES TO KILL HIM

As far as I can recall, Columbia, the capital city of South Carolina, has not been given to fighting labor unions. I was there many times during strikes of textile workers, or before Labor Board elections, and never saw any violence done union people. The police were law-abiding and friendly. The two papers had better attitudes toward the CIO than the average southern paper. George Buchanan, editor of the *Columbia Record,* was always a constructive influence and fair in his attitude. The Textile Union locals in Columbia had secured agreements with managements long years ago and these had continually been renewed.

Yet in 1949, John V. Riffe, director of the CIO Southern Organizing Committee and a resident of Atlanta, was brutally attacked in a hall on the outskirts of Columbia, S. C. The following is an account by William H. Crawford, who was present at the time.

"On the night of March 4, 1949, the members of our union, then on strike against the Shakespeare Company at Columbia, South Carolina, gathered for an evening of social enjoyment in an upstairs hall on the outskirts of Columbia.

"Our members and their families, among their number being many young children, came together to partake of refreshments, hear reports from their strike leaders, spending the latter part of the evening singing and dancing. It was a perfectly orderly crowd with no hint of rowdyism, one that our union could be proud of.

"Among the visitors and union leaders present were southern-drive staff man Glen Earp and his wife, steel representative Lawrence Marine and wife, director of District 35 of the Steelworkers W. H. Crawford and his wife, international representatives of the Steelworkers John G. Ramsey and John V. Riffe. John Riffe was well thought of by all the workers then on strike but the company felt different about John and vague threats had been spread around. However, no one that night had the slightest inkling of what was to follow.

"The evening of fun and entertainment was drawing to a close, the union's representatives had bade goodbye to the strikers and their families, the musicians had packed their instruments and departed; no one was left but John Riffe and the families of the strikers for whom John had kindly offered to provide transportation in order that they could come to the meeting.

"John had already filled his car two times and taken our people home. He returned to the hall for his third and final car load when a gang of hoodlums swarmed up the stairs and without provocation assaulted John Riffe, leaving him as they thought a dead man.

"Shortly after arriving at a local hotel, I was called by phone by one of our people to assist in getting John to the hospital. His skull was fractured in several places, he was cut and bruised all over, he appeared more dead than alive. Fortunately, his strong will and fine physique triumphed over this ghastly attempt at murder, and we are thankful today that John Riffe is in a much higher position in the labor movement and is still able to carry on the fight for our unions."

NO BILL OF RIGHTS IN MEMPHIS, TENNESSEE

Over a period of years it was not safe for a CIO representative to go into Memphis. Organizers from outside who were bold enough to carry the union message to unorganized workers in Memphis paid for it dearly.

Norman Smith, local representative of the United Automobile Workers of America, was a courageous and persistent man who at considerable cost to himself spent some time in the late summer of 1937 preaching the union gospel to the employees of the Ford Assembly plant, one of the largest industries in Memphis at that time. He promptly ran into trouble.

In September, 1937, Mayor Watkins Overton announced in a statement to the press, "We have started today and will free Memphis of these unwanted people. Imported CIO agitators, Communists and highly paid professional organizers are not wanted in Memphis."

Police Commissioner Clifford Davis, referring to Mayor Overton's edict, announced, "We will not tolerate foreign agitators. We know Norman Smith and his whereabouts and will take care of that situation."

Two days after the papers carried that story, Norman Smith was set upon and beaten by a gang of thugs as he left a café. Whereupon he was arrested and held without charges for hours by the police force. Finally he was released. No charges were filed against him, but the beating had injured him so severely that he had to go to a hospital for treatment of scalp wounds and an injured arm. When I saw Smith not long after this brutal attack his head was still swathed in bandages.

Commenting on the obvious cooperation between the police and the industrial interests who wanted to get Smith out of Memphis, an editorial of September 22, 1937, in the *Chattanooga Times* reviewed the abuses of civil rights in Norman Smith's case. Said the editor in his closing words:

The latter-day advocates of State rights and local self-government lose a large part of their argument when it becomes apparent, as it threatens to become in Memphis, that only the Federal Government can protect civil rights under the Constitution.

Smith told me of an earlier incident when he had been decoyed into a dark, lonely street—ostensibly to meet a group of Ford workers who wanted to talk organization. There his car had been surrounded by a group of men who had threatened to kill him unless he left Memphis. Some of them had taken hold of his car and threatened to overturn it and beat him up, but some outside interference had prevented this. He told me that since so much unfavorable publicity had been given the Ford Company and its hired thugs, the police had designated a car to follow him wherever he went. A policeman sat in the lobby of his hotel to watch his coming and going and his visitors. While this added to his safety it was also an effective way to keep him from talking to Ford employees.

One night when he went to his second-floor room, before he switched on the light he saw a man standing in the shadow on the sidewalk opposite his window. The man had one hand in his coat pocket as though it held a pistol. Smith stayed in the dark and kept out of range of the window. Next day he moved to a room on a higher floor.

Finally, after Smith had been knocked around and beaten again, his national union insisted that he had taken enough punishment and must be withdrawn from Memphis.

I like to think that Norman Smith came back to Memphis, without fear of thugs or police, to attend an educational conference put on by the United Automobile Workers of America in 1941 as a means of acquainting their membership with the policies and program of the union. That was after the union had won a notable victory in securing a union-management agreement with Ford. Ford workers had lived so long under the bloody domain of Ford's "personnel director," Harry Bennett that they had to learn new techniques in building democratic procedures.

The first CIO union to secure a collective bargaining agreement in Memphis was the American Newspaper Guild. Organization began in 1936 and was brought to a successful conclusion in June, 1937. The first president of the Memphis Guild was Harry Martin, now president of the American Newspaper Guild. Next in the presidency was W. A. Copeland, Memphis man, who served from 1938 to 1940. Another early leader in the Guild was Allan L. Swim. When Van A. Bittner took charge of the CIO's southern drive in June, 1946, Mr. Swim was appointed director of publicity for the drive. Later on he was made editor and publicity director for the *CIO News,* until he went overseas on a mission connected with organized labor.

As Mr. Copeland put it, "The cornerstone of the CIO in Memphis was the local chapter of the Newspaper Guild." Copeland was himself an active CIO promoter and helped organize other unions. He was appointed to the CIO staff as director in the Memphis area on August 1, 1943.

The second CIO union was the Inland Boatmen's Division of the National Maritime Union which grew rapidly. After a successful strike against the Federal Barge Lines in March, 1939, the local officers were active in promoting unions in industrial plants. W. R. Henderson, active in the strike and contract negotiations, became port agent for the Boatmen, and he was with me in many of the organization meetings I attended. Later, because of his energetic volunteer help, he was put on the CIO staff.

Unions grew rapidly in Memphis in the years between 1937 and 1940. Most of them were in rather small plants. There was an apparently well-founded report that accounts for the comparative lack of interference with the organization of these smaller plants by the city administration. Mr. Crump, boss of Memphis and Shelby County, made an agreement with the AF of L that if it would lay off of organizing any large plants—he wanted to attract large industries to Memphis and desired to assure them that they would not be bothered by union efforts to organize their employees—he would protect the AF of L in its promotion of craft unions. Since the CIO, however, went vigorously to work to organize the large as well as the smaller plants, it incurred the special enmity of Mr. Crump. As a result, the city administration and the AF of L jointly fought the CIO.

CIO unions represented working men and women in many plants, including woodworking, chemicals, fertilizers, fabricated steel, automobile parts, feeds and implements used on farms, cotton and cottonseed products. The majority of these workers were colored. Often the CIO representatives had the task of educating white union members to practice no discrimination because of race, creed, or color, something essential if unions were to be soundly based. In Memphis it was easier than usual to get both white and Negroes into the unions right from the beginning, because the white workers realized that without the colored they could not represent the majority needed to build a union.

In the early years of organization in Memphis I visited the city frequently and spoke to many union meetings. At first the only available meeting place was the Inland Boatmen's Hall. It was the last building on an abruptly downhill, dark street ending at the river. One night I recall speaking to steelworkers first, then walking to the Boatmen's Hall. Because of the stories I had heard about unwanted Negroes being shackled and dumped into the Mississippi, the dark water with its broken reflections of lights had a sinister look. I was glad when my walk ended at the Hall.

Typical of the enthusiasm among Memphis workers for the CIO's industrial unions were the responses to gatherings I attended one evening. I had been asked to speak to a new group. The hall and the street were swarming with Negro men in their working clothes. One group was expected, five were there waiting for us. They used the main hall of the little building, the office back of the hall, and three groups of men formed in the street. When the meetings were over, the men gathered together in the hall and overflowed to the street for a joint assembly to hear the speaker.

This was a stirring occasion, a working of democracy at the grass roots, and I was much moved. Looking back across the years it still amazes me that the handful of white union men who led this movement were able to win the confidence of their colored brothers, and how readily the Negroes received the aid of these white men who talked about one union for all the workers in a plant—men and women—white and colored.

Those meetings were deeply religious. A colored member would pray and lead in singing and dismiss the gathering with a blessing. In one group there was an elderly Negro who "lined out" the Lord's prayer verse by verse while the others repeated the words after him. They were praying for more of the Kingdom of God on earth. Sometimes they would ask the white organizer to lead in prayer, and the white man always responded. Sometimes I was the one who prayed and I was always so moved by the spirit of the Negroes that it was hard to steady my voice. I think I never heard people pray more sincerely than did those humble union folk.

I find a few notes made when I was attending union meetings. One earnest brother said: "The company stooge who tells the boss who is a member of this union is taking pork chops off your wife's and children's plates. He is stealing their food. We got to stick together to help us and our families."

Another said: "We must have self-confidence in God. Self-confidence is self-help. We must put our arms around each other and lift each other up. Let us cling together and rise together. Living is God's gift to us. We got to use it right. This union is part of our living and we got to stick by it."

In a packed meeting in a funeral hall a tall, thin man with gray hair dwelt at length on the wonders of the CIO. He said: "This CIO is a great thing—it makes wonderful things happen. After he heard about our union, our boss called some of us in his office—that never happened before. He made us sit down in the big chairs in his office, and he asked us what we wanted, and what would satisfy us. We told him we would have to talk to the committee before we could say what we wanted. He had never asked what we wanted till we had a union."

The union steward said: "The bosses asked us what we wanted so they could keep us from organizing, but they were too late, we had already organized."

The union president said: "I met the boss just after I got out of work and he asked me what was this he heard about our going to organize a union. He said he knew I would tell him the truth about it. And I said 'We *have* organized.' He looked surprised and asked what we want. I told him we would let him know what we want after we had thought about it and made our plans. Then he asked me which way was I going and did I want to get taken home, and I said 'no,' I was not going home yet."

In another meeting, also in a funeral home, a union officer said: "The boss came out in the plant today. He came by me and he stopped and said, 'Are you feeling good?' and I said 'yes.' Then he said, 'How did you like that three cents an hour raise I gave you last week?' I said, 'The committee will talk to you about that.' "

Harry Kroger, once a YMCA secretary, was often with me at these evening meetings. He had a great concern for the depressed and oppressed and a sense of spiritual values. He was especially troubled for the exploited sharecroppers across the river and took me for a long drive in Arkansas. We called in two Negro homes, one was very poor and plain, but clean. The other was nicely furnished, with curtains at the windows and comfortable chairs. The son of this simple woman had somehow gotten an education and was a professional man in a distant city. He kept his mother supplied with necessities and comforts. She was proud of him and spoke of his visits with pleasure.

In the summer of 1940, three years after automobile worker Smith's adventures in Memphis, the mayor and city administration were aroused by the presence of George R. Bass, representative of the United Rubber Workers. In a front page story under the heading "City Closes Doors on Labor Agitators," the *Memphis Commercial Appeal* of August 25, 1940, wrote:

Mayor issues statement after CIO organizer charges he was assailed. "Foreign labor agitators who seek to stir up strife and trouble are not welcome here," Mayor Chandler said yesterday, after Ben F. Baldwin . . . a Firestone employee, had been dismissed in City Court on a charge of disturbing the peace by assailing a United Rubber Workers (CIO) organizer in the Claridge lobby.

The Mayor's statement, serving notice that the Police Department has been warned to prevent any disturbances which may arise out of attempts to unionize the Firestone plant, was interpreted by Acting Chief Seabrook to mean that "lives and property in Memphis must be protected." . . .

Mr. Seabrook said George R. Bass of Akron, Ohio, the CIO organizer, would not be "run out of town as long as he conducts himself properly."

The news story goes on

Mr. Bass yesterday said he is waiting for word from union head-quarters on whether to prosecute Mr. Baldwin for assault and battery. "I don't want to start any trouble here," Mr. Bass said. "I talked those men who said I would end up in the river out of a fight Friday night." Mr. Bass identified some of the men as part-time supervisors at the Firestone plant.

Among other things the mayor had to say about Bass was the following: "Memphis will not tolerate intimidations, or threats of bodily harm to those who wish to work, and foreign labor agitators who seek to stir up strife and trouble are not welcome here."

In reply Bass pointed out that he was born in Tennessee and was not a "foreigner." He also pointed out that all attacks had been made upon him while he was quietly trying to carry out his work of acquainting the Firestone workers with the benefits of unionism.

In a short time Bass had made real progress in organizing the Firestone plant, but in that time he had been turned out of hotel rooms, been refused accommodation in the rest of the hotels, required to leave an apartment where he had found a room, and attacked at various times. He finally managed to get a room in an obscure place and went on with his work.

I recall driving about Memphis on the front seat of Mr. Bass' car while one of the plant employees who had come on the Rubber

Workers staff to aid in protecting him sat alert on the back seat with
a pistol in his pocket. Bass was a strongly built man, with thick,
wavy black hair and black eyes. He never used a weapon and no
one on the Firestone side was ever injured because of his efforts to
organize the workers.

I was in the union office (they were using the Inland Boatmen's
Hall near the river) with Bass and some other man when two young
white men came in and asked for Bass. Bass identified himself and
asked what he could do for them. One of them said,

"Is it true that Niggers will be taken in this union?"

Bass recognized the significance of this question, but promptly
said "Yes." The two men were obviously angry. They left in a min-
ute or two. Bass then said their visit meant that the AF of L was
stirring up the race issue in the plant and the CIO people would be
hearing from it. "It will probably cost us the election," he said.

Bass and his helpers were handing out leaflets at the plant a day
or two later, with police standing by and looking on, when a mob
of employees jumped on them and beat Bass so severely that he had
to be rushed to the hospital in a CIO man's car. There he spent
several days.

Bass and his associates came near death not long after that. He
thought he had found a room in an apartment house and had started
to move into it with the help of two assistants, when the owner told
him he could not have him in his house. Bass' car was parked outside. When he and his assistants came out and got into it, it would
not start. While he was still trying to start it, a band of thugs arrived
and surrounded them. The Ford plant supervisor with the thugs
ordered them to turn the car over—which they did. They wrecked
the car, using lead pipes, 2 by 4 planks, and hose. They then turned
the car on its back with the three men still inside. One managed to
crawl out the back and ran to call the police. Bass and one companion could not get out because the crushed top of the car had bound
the front doors shut. Bass managed at last to crawl over into the
back of the car, to open a door and get out. While in the car he saw
a man take the gasoline cap off and when the gas had poured on the

ground the man struck a match and tried to set it afire, but for some reason it did not ignite.

When the three men were all on the outside of the car, a squad car arrived with two policemen. The car was a complete wreck, beyond repair. The police made Bass have it hauled away, though he wanted it to remain until the gang that wrecked it had been discovered.

All of this time, officers of the union, and others, including myself, were trying to get the Department of Justice to intervene in the interest of preserving civil rights to men who were being violently denied them. It seemed impossible to get any action from the District Attorney or the Department of Justice. I spent most of one day trying to see Boss Crump. After I had spent hours sitting in Mr. Crump's outer office, hoping he would come in or go out so that I could speak to him, his secretary told me that he was in town but I could not see him—evidently he had another means of access to his office.

Mr. Crump was a Democratic National Committeeman. It occurred to me that I might use this as a means of reaching the President—Mr. Crump was flouting the Democratic Party platform in making war on unions; furthermore, he was turning Democrats into Republicans, or Socialists, or even Communists as he persecuted union people.

So, after returning to Atlanta, I wrote a desperate letter to Mrs. Roosevelt, asking her help. She wired suggesting that we lunch together in New York after attending a national woman's forum to be held there. We had lunch together on November 26, 1940, and I told her the story. She asked me to make a brief report on the Memphis situation, mail it to her quickly, and she would put it in the President's private letterbox by his bed. After he had read the report she would talk to him about the situation. The answer came in an unexpected manner.

Early in January, Colonel Amos W. Woodcock appeared in Memphis as a special representative of the Attorney General to look into charges against the city administration concerning the denial of civil rights to union people.

The Memphis papers reported that U. S. District Attorney Mc-Clanahan and City Commissioner Joe Boyle, on both of whom Colonel Woodcock called, assured him that if there had been any violations of civil rights they did not know of them. They also promised the Colonel that whatever might have happened in the past there would be no such violations in the future.

Naturally this sudden interest in protecting civil rights on the part of federal and city representatives had a most salutary effect. There were no repetitions of incidents similar to those experienced by Smith and Bass. CIO people could come and go unmolested. Unions grew rapidly.

W. A. Copeland wrote me in May, 1951, that he estimated there were 30,000 CIO members in Memphis.

Two mayors of Memphis who had for a period of years sought to destroy the CIO had great changes of heart after the CIO had become firmly established in their city.

The Memphis *Press-Scimitar* of June, 1942, carried a favorable front-page story about the convention of the Tennessee Industrial Union Council. Part of the story was devoted to side remarks by reporters recalling the mayor's one-time hatred for the CIO. But much more space was given to praising the same CIO. Here is an excerpt from Mayor Chandler's address:

"I have had experience with the CIO in Washington. I have followed with interest the program of the CIO. It is a very interesting movement. I have met your leaders in Washington. I have always found them courteous and it was an agreeable relationship. You are genuinely welcome here."

Nine years later, in the fall of 1950, my friend Bill Crawford, director of the southeastern district of the United Steelworkers of America, gleefully told me about Mayor Watkin Overton's address of welcome when the union held its convention in Memphis that year.

Mayor Overton spoke enthusiastically of the part the CIO had played in the development and improvement of the city. He praised the CIO members as good citizens. To cap the climax, the mayor said, "As you raise the standards of living of your members, you raise the standards of living of everybody in the South."

TIFTON, GEORGIA: THEY CALLED US WHITE TRASH

In the spring of 1948, Grover R. Hathaway, director of the southeastern district of the United Packing House Workers of America, requested me to go to Tifton, Georgia, to look into the violations of civil rights of striking packing house workers. The acting sheriff was undertaking to get striking workers back into the Armour Company plant at Tifton by threats and violence. I arrived by train about six o'clock Sunday afternoon and went directly to the home of Jake Watson, secretary-treasurer of the local union.

There I found some of the local union men and also Joe Moore, of the CIO staff, who had come in some weeks before to help the Tifton people. Joe is a short man, with an honest, kindly face. He lost a leg in the coal mines many years ago, but his lameness has not kept him from taking all sorts of hard and dangerous assignments. He is as plucky as he is devoted to the labor movement.

Having gotten all I could about the strike, and discussed the next day's job, I went to the hotel and got a good rest, which was fortunate as Jake Watson called me at 6:30 next morning to come to his house and talk with a Negro striker who had been man-handled by the sheriff and a plant guard the night before.

When I got to Watson's home I found the man with swollen jaw, cheeks, and eyes. He could not write and so I took down his story and he was able to put his name to it. I do not use his name lest it should be prejudicial to him some day—let's call him George.

Though I shall refer to the acting sheriff as the "sheriff," actually he was filling the unexpired term of the sheriff who had died in office. The sheriff-elect would not take office for some months. He was generally regarded as a fine young man, well equipped for his job. (At the time I am writing, that sheriff has been in office several years and has made a good record.)

The story George told me was that he had just gotten back from church and pulled off his coat when there was a knock at the front door. When he opened the door, there stood one of the Armour plant guards.

In his car in front of the house sat the sheriff. The plant guard told George that he and the sheriff wanted to talk with him in the car. They put him on the front seat with the sheriff, and the guard sat on the back seat and mauled the poor fellow's face with his fist. They took him for a long drive, and in an isolated spot in the woods stopped the car. They threatened George with more physical injury and the burning of his house if he did not go back to work in the plant next day and take all the other striking Negro workers with him. He did not make any promises.

When I had gotten from George the statement to be sent to the Civil Rights Section of the Department of Justice, I went on a search for the sheriff. Usually I go alone to talk with officers who have violated someone's civil rights, for they will talk more freely in private. But staunch Joe Moore insisted on going along, as did J. C. Bradshaw, secretary-treasurer of the local union, and Richard Luke, president.

Not finding the sheriff, I went to see Judge R. Eve of the local court. Judge Eve and I had a bond in common, since we are both members of the Franklin D. Roosevelt Warm Springs Memorial Commission. I told him the story and he said that he would get a message to the sheriff to be at the judge's office at four o'clock. Until the appointed hour I spent the day calling on the chief of police, business men, and ministers.

At four o'clock I went back to Judge Eve's office and found him alone. His office and the sheriff's were nearly opposite, with a wide hall between. Hearing angry voices I hurried into the hall. There the sheriff and three deputies, all with guns sticking out of their hip pockets, faced Bradshaw, Moore and Luke, none of whom was armed. Hot words were being exchanged.

The judge did not come out of his office, but I am sure that the fact that he was within hearing distance, with his door opening into the hall near us, prevented real trouble.

I entered into the verbal fray by trying to make the sheriff understand he had flouted federal guarantees of civil rights. He threw his arms above his head and poured imprecations on me. He said he wished I was a man so he could tell me what he thought of me. He made that very clear! He said he knew Tift County law and that was all he needed to know.

He asked how I knew anything about him. When I told him that I had been inquiring into his conduct since I arrived the evening before, he glowered at me and shouted, "And I been having you watched ever since you got off that train yesterday. You been associating with niggers and white trash—you ain't seen no decent people since you got here."

The sheriff was especially angry with Joe Moore, saying he had made all the trouble by coming in from Atlanta and stirring up union talk. He was threatening to Joe and told him he ought to go back to Atlanta.

The air became electric, touched off by the words "white trash." My three companions moved toward the sheriff—Mr. Bradshaw had his fists doubled, ready for attack. He and Luke shouted, "Can't anybody call me white trash." Wise and experienced Joe Moore was trying to pull the other two back. I do not know what would have happened if I had not stepped between the opposing forces. It would have been bad for our men if one of them had laid a finger on the sheriff.

I stood with my back to the sheriff and my hands on the shoulders of Bradshaw and Luke, pushing them back and urging them to leave the building and go away in their car. I appealed to Joe Moore to get them out. All the time I laughed saying, "Why do you care what he calls you—that is just funny."

Afterwards the men told me if I had not kept smiling they would have sailed into the sheriff—and probably been killed.

What also helped was that I told our men they must get away from there so that I could telephone U. S. District Attorney John

Cowart at Macon, and ask him to have an immediate investigation of civil rights violations in Tifton. Bluff as he would, the sheriff was afraid of "the government," to which his acts were to be reported.

When the CIO men had gone to their car, I was left with four armed men. The younger deputies looked a bit sheepish at this array of strength against one old woman, and went back to their office. Left together, the sheriff and I stared at each other in silence. He yielded by going out to his car, parked just opposite the CIO car. He got in and turned to watch our men. To be on the safe side I walked down to the street and watched the two cars. In a few minutes our men drove off, then the sheriff followed suit.

That night the sheriff and his deputies roamed the Negro district in their police cars—we did the same in CIO cars. But no incident took place—that night or thereafter during the strike. The federal government must have loomed large in the sheriff's mind.

After phoning the District Attorney at Macon, I returned to Judge Eve's office and accepted his hospitality and typewriter in writing charges against the sheriff covering denials of civil rights. The FBI made an investigation and the sheriff's behavior became perfect.

The national Packing House Workers' strike was brought to a conclusion; the striking workers went back to the plant; the sheriff had sought solace on his farm; George was one of the first men given his job, and he needed it, with a wife and ten children to support. So the matter ended without prosecution, but satisfactorily.

GILES COUNTY, VIRGINIA

Way up in the northwest section of Virginia there is a little town called Narrows, situated in a lovely valley beside a pretty river, with mountains on each side. Five miles from Narrows is Pearisburg, and halfway between the two towns by the river is a large plant of the Celanese Corporation of America.

Pearisburg is located in Giles County—the courthouse is there, and also the offices of the Celanese plant.

My trip to Narrows was made at the request of Ernest B. Pugh, CIO Virginia state director, to stop the illegal arrests of CIO representatives for distributing leaflets at the entrance of the Celanese plant while shifts were changing.

When the local train brought me into Narrows that October afternoon in 1948, the sun-bathed red and gold mountains, the rippling river, and the deep blue sky were beautiful to behold. As the hotel belonged to the Celanese Corporation, I could not get a room there and drove with one of the CIO men to another town and hotel about thirty miles away. So I had an opportunity to refresh my soul with mountain beauty while I combated the corporation which reigned supreme in economic affairs.

We had a staff meeting in the CIO office in Narrows the night of my arrival. Lloyd Vaughan, Virginia director for the Textile Workers Union of America, was there; also W. V. Vanover, of the CIO staff, Murphy George and Cobey Snyder. Months before, when four CIO men had handed out union leaflets at the Celanese plant, they had been arrested for trespassing on company property. Their cases had never been settled and the men were still under bond. Further leaflet distributing might lead to more arrests. I quote from the complaint made to the Civil Rights Section of the Department of Justice in this case:

The distributions were made on the roadway by which busses and private cars bring employees to work, and which circles around in front of the main entrance to the plant; also on the walkway used by the people as they come in from bus or car, or by those who walked to work. There is a parking space marked "public parking" just to the side of this road and the union people stand on the edge of that also.

In these approaches the company property adjoins or merges with the public highway and parking lot. It was in circumstances similar to these that the Supreme Court decided in favor of CIO unions in the cases of the National Labor Relations Board versus LeTourneau Company of Georgia, and also in the case of Republic Aviation Corporation versus the NLRB. The law was clearly on the union's side.

We had a staff meeting the night I arrived and it was decided to make distributions at the changes of shift next day. Four of the men were on hand at six o'clock the next morning, and while they were handing out leaflets, a plant personnel man came out and asked their names. Three gave fictitious names, while the fourth promptly left for his home in another county.

In preparation for the afternoon activities, I spent the morning seeing the Narrows banker, courthouse people, some ministers, and especially Sheriff Emory Johnston. The sheriff seemed to be correctly informed as to the right of the union men to distribute leaflets in this situation. He assured us that he believed they had this right, but that he could not decide whether or not he would serve warrants —in that matter he had to do as he was ordered by the justice of the peace and the commonwealth's attorney, J. C. Stafford.

At three o'clock the men and I went to the Celanese plant to hand out more leaflets. I took an active part in this and was the last to leave the plant gate. The sheriff appeared and went into the plant. A personnel man came out and asked our names, which we gave him correctly. All went well and we were not disturbed until the distribution was over and the workers back in the plant.

As we were getting into our cars the sheriff and a Virginia highway patrolman came up and the sheriff said he had four warrants to serve. He and the patrolman were friendly. When it developed that three of the names on the sheriff's warrants were not known to us, and the fourth man had gone home to his family in another county, the sheriff said he was not going chasing all over the county looking for men that nobody seemed to know.

Messrs. Vaughan and Vanover then went with me to look for J. C. Stafford, commonwealth's attorney, who had been out of town all day.

As we walked through the wide courthouse hall I saw a young man coming up the path. He was a pleasant looking young fellow, with a likable, honest face. I extended my hand and asked if he was Mr. Stafford, and he was. I told him I had tried to save him some trouble with the Department of Justice by finding him earlier. He was most courteous, but mystified by my reference to trouble and asked what he had been doing that was wrong.

When I told him about civil rights and the violations of them by the arrests he had caused to be made, he said,

"I don't know any federal laws, I just know about Giles County and Virginia laws. I can't be blamed for what I don't know."

We had a half-laughing conversation on the possible consequences of his denials of civil rights by having our men arrested on request of the Celanese Corporation's attorney. I assured him that I did not want to see him go to jail or pay a large fine—we just wanted him to let our people exercise their constitutional and statutory rights of free speech—in this case involved in handing out leaflets.

Mr. Stafford and I got on the subject of his ancestors, who had been bold pioneers from Tide-water Virginia to the mountains, while mine had settled in or near the Tide-water section. I told him about George Mason and the Bill of Rights in both the Virginia and federal constitutions.

He seemed mild and reasonable and I told him I had to have copies of the warrants which the sheriff had tried to serve that morning, since it was customary to make a report of this sort of thing to the Department of Justice as a background in case there was further similar trouble. He said I could get the warrants from the printer's office next morning—it was now nearing six o'clock. I asked him to get them for me right then and there, but he hung back and said I would be able to get them next day. Being unsure of this, I caught his arm in mine, wheeled him around and together we walked to the printer's office, where he secured the blank warrants. He then insisted on taking me to the sheriff's office to have the warrants properly filled in. I told him I had met the sheriff and he knew about federal guarantees of civil rights.

We parted amicably and I assured him that I expected no further trouble—he said indeed there would not be. Thereafter, the CIO representatives were not interfered with when handing out union leaflets at the Celanese plant.

As we went to the car, Vanover joined Vaughan and me. He had been listening to my conversation with Mr. Stafford and observing the highway patrolman we had met earlier, who was hidden behind a large tree and convulsed with laughter over my talk with Mr. Stafford. As Stafford and I walked off to the printer's office arm-in-arm, the patrolman said to Vanover, "I don't mean any disrespect, but I do hope that old lady will give him hell."

When Vaughan and I drove away he said to me, "I never understood before why the CIO had a lady handling civil rights, but I do now. If I had talked to that attorney like you did and put my arm in his to get him to the printer's office, he would have knocked me down."

There were no further denials of free speech at Narrows.

TALLAPOOSA, GEORGIA

Though it hardly seems necessary to add another to the accounts of lawless conduct by employers directed against union members, I am including one more. It is the story of Burnell and Earlene Rochester, union members, employed in the American Thread Mill at Tallapoosa, Georgia—one of many mills owned by the same company.

This account is developed in detail in the hearings before the Sub-committee on Labor-Management Relations of the Committee on Labor and Public Welfare, U. S. Senate. Senator James E. Murray was chairman of this Sub-committee, and the hearings began August 21, 1950.

This is the second episode of violence to go before the National Labor Relations Board involving the American Thread Mill at Tallapoosa. The first was that of Mrs. Edna Martin, of Athens, Georgia, organizer for the Textile Workers Union, who was taken from her room in a rooming house in Tallapoosa at midnight November 17, 1947, by a gang of nine people headed by one Elza Teal. Mrs. Martin's hands were tied and she was forced into the back of a truck. After a long, cold drive she was dumped like a sack of meal onto a dirt road a long way from anywhere.

The victim of the kidnapping was so sprained and bruised that I went with her to see Dr. Randolph Smith when she came to the

TWUA office on November 19. I also took Mrs. Martin's statement describing exactly what happened to her and it was used at the Senate Committee hearing.

A little later I helped in the search for witnesses to prove that the plant superintendent knew of and connived in the kidnapping. We thought we had the evidence, but the Labor Board disagreed with us. The Martin case was widely publicized at the time and we were greatly disappointed that the NLRB failed to sustain the charges against the American Thread Company's Tallapoosa management.

In the Rochesters' cases the Labor Board made a sweeping decision sustaining the union charges against the company's management and ordering it to cease and desist from its anti-union practices.

Notwithstanding opposition by the company and some of its employees, union members from the organized plant at Dalton had been visiting the unorganized workers at Tallapoosa. The Dalton people had gained a great deal in wages, improved working conditions, and other union benefits, and sought all opportunities to acquaint the Tallapoosa workers with these union advantages.

So it was that on August 2, 1949, four union members from Dalton went to Tallapoosa to hand out leaflets to the workers there. They started distribution shortly before the change in shifts. Fifteen minutes before the shift whistle blew seven men came from the plant to the public street where the union members were standing, and approached them, brandishing clubs and cursing them violently. The union people tried to reason with the men, but were threatened with their lives if they did not leave the plant gates immediately. Naturally they withdrew. They went down town and told a policeman what had happened and asked him to intervene in behalf of their rights. Said the upholder of the law, "I don't want a damn thing to do with your kind of business."

The leaders of this anti-union mob were Elza Teal (hero in the kidnapping of Mrs. Edna Martin) and his stalwart son Durward, a man of tall and large frame, who chose victims of smaller size.

Like other missionaries who believe in their cause, the union people in Dalton continued to visit Tallapoosa and attempt to distribute union leaflets. On August 4, 1949, the union members who had had to retreat two days earlier gathered unto themselves several other union friends and went back to Tallapoosa to try to finish the job of distributing union papers.

Shortly before the change of shift at three o'clock, a group of mill employees gathered on plant property and talked with H. M. Woods, an overseer of the Company. Just as the whistle blew the group— without the overseer—and others totalling about twenty came out of the mill gate led by Durward Teal. He was carrying a double-barreled shotgun and Elza Teal was brandishing a pistol. They pointed their guns at the union members, swore at them, and threatened to kill them if they did not leave at once.

A city policeman, sitting in his car within twenty feet of the scene, refused to take any part in checking this lawless behavior. The union men had no choice other than to leave.

The next attempt to hand out union papers was made by one man alone, Burnell Rochester. Mr. Rochester was a union member from Tallapoosa. He had a supply of the *Georgia News Digest,* a labor paper, and had decided to distribute these to the employees of the American Thread Plant.

On August 19, Rochester was standing in front of the company gate with his papers, at shift-change time, when Durward Teal walked out of the plant and assaulted him with his fists. After knocking Rochester to the ground he pounced on top of him and continued to beat him about the face.

Earlene Rochester, Burnell's wife, who also works in the Tallapoosa plant, is a small but plucky woman and undertook to pull Teal off of her husband. Teal got up and slugged her with his fists— finally knocking her unconscious.

Throughout this occasion, our hero, Elza Teal, Durward's father, used his shotgun—which he had brought out from the mill—and verbal threats to kill, to prevent any one from coming to the aid of Mrs. Rochester, even threatening to kill anyone who picked her up from the street. When warrants for assault and battery and pointing a gun were sworn out against the Teals, prominent community leaders gave bond for this lawless pair.

There are pages of this sort of testimony in the Labor Board trial examiner's report, plus the testimony of witnesses at the Washington committee hearing. This testimony showed without possibility of refutation that the plans to attack the union people were made inside the plant, with company officials assisting. And so the Labor Board found.

DUBLIN, GEORGIA—JAIL AND COSTS

Most incredible, perhaps, is the fact that these incidents continue down to the present day. Often they get scant attention by the press and none by the legally constituted local authorities.

For instance, when on a chilly night in February, 1951, Charles H. Gillman, CIO state director, and Clyde Brock, also of the CIO staff, were suddenly arrested while attending a union meeting in Dublin, Georgia, the press gave little attention to the matter.

Brock and Gillman had gone to Dublin in response to a request for help in forming a union among the woodworkers of that area. The sheriff and two deputies came into the meeting and promptly arrested the two men. The sheriff had two of his deputies take them to jail without warrants or charges. Both men were denied opportunity to get in touch with their office and their homes. They spent a sleepless night in a filthy jail.

Next morning about eleven o'clock a local lawyer appeared and examined the men's identification, which included Masonic cards. This lawyer then called Oral Garrison, secretary-treasurer of the CIO Organizing Committee in Atlanta, who arranged to make whatever bond was necessary.

Mr. Garrison called Hugo Black, in Birmingham, one of the attorneys representing the CIO. Mr. Black arranged with the Dublin lawyer to comply with whatever was necessary to get the two men released at once. But a judge to hear the case had to be brought in from a distance and it was six o'clock before the men were set free.

The judge set a sum of $200 "for attorney fees and costs," which

Mr. Black had to wire from Birmingham. More than twenty hours in a dirty jail and a total cost of $200 was the punishment of two totally innocent men—their offense, attending a peaceful union meeting!

The only light thrown on the matter are two statements by the sheriff as reported in the papers, who said he asked:

"Is this a meeting of the Jehovah Witnesses? Is this a Communist meeting?" Receiving no answer, said the sheriff, he had the men jailed.

Apparently trying to connect the CIO men with communism the sheriff said, according to the press, that

shortly before, he had attended an FBI school and was told to be alert for persons who might be connected with communism.

Gillman and Brock have been in the forefront of the fight against communism within and without the labor union movement. Brock is a veteran—both are natives of the deep South.

Chapter V

LEADERSHIP

THE MEN I have called leaders in this book are among those I have known from my early days with the CIO. They are inherently strong men, and their experiences in the labor movement have caused them to develop leadership.

Varied qualities are needed for union leadership, and basic to all else is integrity, for without that the leader cannot hold the confidence of the union people, or the respect of the public. After that, come imagination and wisdom and courage and an unprejudiced mind, and a deep concern for the welfare of the people with whom he works.

These men and those described elsewhere in these pages had them all.

MEN IN STEEL

Ernest Starnes

The penetration of industrial unionism into the South has worked many wonders. None, it seems to me, is more wonderful than the new respect and understanding between races which had been separated for generations by law and tradition.

It was in the Atlantic Steel plant in Atlanta, one of the focal points in the CIO's regional drive, that a major turning point was reached on the question of working together for a common cause.

The significance of the incident can hardly be overestimated. Because of its size alone, the Atlantic Steelworkers' local was an important center of activity. Added to that was the makeup of the local membership. Nearly 40 per cent were Negro. Whatever happened there, on the practical level of day-to-day operation, would have a far-reaching effect.

When W. H. Crawford became District 35 director for steel, he found that the Atlantic local, unlike the others, held separate meetings for white and colored.

"Each Saturday morning the white members would meet in one section of the city," Bill Crawford explained. "Then, in the afternoon, the officers of the local, who were all white, attended a meeting in the colored section to inform the Negro members of the action taken at the morning meeting.

"This procedure was undemocratic, unworkable, and completely at variance with the aims and policies of the Steelworkers.

"My first contact with the aggressive leadership of this local union led me to depend on its president, R. E. Starnes.

"In one of the first meetings, Starnes made the statement to me that if he and I could see eye to eye we would do a job of organizing in Atlanta.

"I asked him what he meant by that statement. He then said that we would have to keep the Negroes and white people separate in all the locals we established. I informed him that the waste of money involved in such a procedure would result in my being fired by the International on the standpoint of cost alone. Then I explained the policy and program of the Steelworkers along these lines.

"After Starnes attended the 1942 convention and returned to Atlanta, he informed me that he could see what we were trying to do now, and he was with me wholeheartedly. After seeing what went on at the convention, Starnes realized the economic futility and the unfairness of attempting to organize separate locals for white and colored.

"After several months passed, with Starnes and me working together on the officers and members of the local, we were able to get them to pass a resolution abandoning separate meetings."

In introducing Ernie Starnes through Bill Crawford's statement, I have been trying to do two things: first, to give some idea of Ernie's quality and worth as a leader in the union movement in the South, and second, to present Ernie as a symbol of the movement. He is a born-and-bred-in-the-brier-patch southerner, and I think that it can truly be said that "as Ernie Starnes goes, so goes the South."

I first met him in the SWOC office a day or two after the Atlantic Steel strike began in 1941. As president of the local union he carried a great deal of responsibility.

He stuck to his job day and night. He was always there, on the spot, and it was due to his level head and good judgment that there were not some bad incidents.

Ernie is a natural leader, direct and forceful in his decisions and actions, and yet he is a singularly gentle man. In searching for the right description of him, it occurred to me that I would have to contrast his strong, honest face with the smile which often appears there. One morning I said to him, "Ernie, I can't write about you without mentioning your smile. It's a shy smile. Do you mind?"

He looked up, and there it was again. "I reckon not," he said. "Not if you can't help yourself." And really, I couldn't help myself. Without that smile, it wouldn't be Ernie.

He spent the last six years of his plant employment as a finisher. It is one of the most demanding and dangerous jobs in industry. A finisher handles hot steel with tongs gripped in his bare hands. As Ernie describes the job, "The finisher catches a bar of hot steel with tongs as it comes out of one set of rolls and swings it around in an arc to another set of rolls. Hot iron is running around you all the time. If a man misses the bar, or the bar misses contact with the second set of rolls, it goes wild, springs up or out, and wraps itself around his body, or head, or legs. That means quick death.

"Once something went wrong and the bar jumped up above my head. I threw up my hands to push it way from my head, and my cap saved my head by a small fraction of an inch. My hands were right badly burned and I had to go to the hospital.

"That bar of steel cuts off and burns anything it wraps around. Once I saw a bar get loose and burn a man's leg clear off.

"There have been a lot of improvements in this process and many safety devices have been developed, so it is not as dangerous as it used to be, but it is still a dangerous job and it is hard to get men to go on it."

"Wouldn't gloves help?" I asked.

"No, they might catch on fire," he replied. "And you can do the job better with bare hands, as they are sensitive to feel when anything goes wrong with the bar in the rolls or as it comes out."

I have been with Ernie on some hazardous assignments, and never have I seen him run away from danger.

He was born in Atlanta in 1915. His mother was a seamstress who belonged to the ILGWU, "and when they struck, she struck." His father was a machinist. One of his brothers became a Baptist minister—"all my folks are Baptists"—and was a Chaplain in the European Theater during World War II.

Ernie's first job was as a messenger, in 1932, the same year when he went as far as Fredericksburg, Virginia, on the Hunger March on Washington.

He had completed the eighth grade, and after a stay in the Civilian Conservation Corps he got out to continue his education. He had been sending his mother twenty-five dollars a month out of his total earnings of thirty dollars in CCC, and it was not long before her need for support sent him back to work. In 1934 he took a job as laborer in the Hoop Mill of the Atlantic Steel Company.

His starting pay was 19 cents an hour. After turns on the cotton tie buckle machine, and as a troughboy, strander, and lay-over man, he became a finisher. This was the top-rated job in the plant, except for roller.

"Talk about a union started in 1939," Ernie said. "There was all sorts of intimidation and coercion against the movement. They even brought forth a newspaper picture showing John L. Lewis having beat up a man in Chicago.

"Late that year, Sam Stephens passed out SWOC literature. Then

Philip Murray sent a full-time representative, Joe Gaither. The first
woman I saw at a union meeting was Lucy Mason."

In response to this, I said, "The first time I saw you, Ernest, was
in Gaither's office. I was working on a news story about the strike.
Gaither told me not to go on the picket line, because it was rough.
Of course, when I left the office I drove directly to the picket line,
parked my car, and went around talking to the men."

It was a bitter strike. Striking for recognition, for its first contract,
the local was forced to improvise its strategy and to act on impulse
at times. Ernie recalls that one of the scabs, a white man named
Grimes, got into the plant and out again through a sewer.

"Four of us went to the mouth of the sewer to watch. After two
days of waiting, the man was caught. I was not there at the time. The
men brought him to me at the union office. We took the man to a
drive-in and bought him a coke. After we told him he wouldn't be
hurt if he kept quiet, we talked to him and found out everything we
wanted to know about conditions inside the plant—the names of
people scabbing, what departments were trying to operate, how
much food they had to eat, and what kind of beds they were sleeping
on, how many women were coming in, and how they were coming in.

"We talked to him about four hours, and then drove him to within
two blocks of his home. We did him no damage, and he said that
he would tell no one about this affair.

"But apparently the police were waiting, because they swore out
a warrant and arrested me no more than three hours later. I was
carried to Fulton County Jail and sentenced to sixty days without
bond by Judge Carpenter. The law firm of Presswood and Hall got
me released two days later on two thousand five hundred dollars bail.

"We had managed to keep trucks and railroad cars from deliver-
ing food to the scabs inside the plant, until the company got an injunction against the railroad and made them put two cars of food on
the company's spur track.

"Just as the company sent out the dinkey engine to haul in the
food, five hundred of us lined up in front of the cars. Fulton County

Police Captain Oliver and five or six other policemen stood on top of the cars with tear gas and sub-machine guns.

"They said they had orders to get the food in, and they were going to do it. They brandished their sub-machine guns and threatened us with the tear gas. We wouldn't move off the tracks. I told them that if anything happened, they might get some of us, but we would get some of them, too.

"I sent word in to the company that if the cars were moved in, it would be over my dead body. In about fifteen minutes, the company sent back word to call it off. The food cars were shipped back to the yards."

There were other incidents, but the strike ended with recognition won for the union. The new contract was sub-standard on seniority, and needed other improvements, but it was only another ninety days before negotiations were reopened.

"We were gradually realizing what the Negroes had meant to us in the strike," Ernie continued.

"We had about six hundred Negro workers and about eight hundred white. A handful of Communists kept up turmoil because of the separate meetings, and, on the other hand, the Ku Klux Klan was harassing us because of our close affiliation with the Negroes.

"We wanted to do the right thing. White and colored were on the picket line together and worked together in the plant all the time. There ought to be just one meeting where everybody could come.

"I realized strongly that we would have gone under without the support of the Negro membership. Out of approximately six hundred people who scabbed the plant, only twelve or fourteen were colored. If the Negroes had gone in to work, our strike would have been lost. I repeatedly told this to the membership, and gradually the situation began to change.

"When the members voted to abandon separate meetings, it was the real thing. All of us had learned a lesson that can never be forgotten."

There is a happy postscript to the bitterness of the 1941 strike at Atlantic Steel.

This story was told me by both R. S. Lynch, president of the company, and W. H. Crawford, director of the United Steelworkers of America in this district. During the Atlanta Community Chest campaign of 1951, Mr. Crawford and Mr. Lynch spoke to the plant's employees in behalf of the Community Chest—both took the occasion to speak of the excellent relations between management and union.

Thanks to the cooperation of company and union, the employees made top-notch records in contributing to the Community Chest, in giving to the blood bank, and in buying war bonds. A laudatory editorial about these contributions in the *Atlanta Journal* gave credit to both union and company.

Mr. Lynch said that cooperation by the workers had made it possible in 1951 to reach the largest production in the history of the Atlantic Steel Company. As a result the company is greatly expanding the capacity of the plant. Five hundred new men will be employed.

In recognition of the union's cooperation, the National Labor Relations Board's help will not be required in order to extend the bargaining unit to cover all employees. All present employees will be advanced according to seniority.

W. H. Crawford

One of the outstanding union stalwarts in SWOC's history in the South is a tall, fine-looking man with iron gray hair and blue eyes—William H. Crawford. When I think of the formative years of the United Steelworkers in the Birmingham area, I think of Bill Crawford. Believing there would be an interesting story here, I asked him to tell me about his experiences. This is his story. There is a tinge of wholesome pride in Bill Crawford's voice as he says: "My father was a pioneer who helped organize the coal mines. I was born in the Hocking Valley, Ohio, in 1888 and entered the coal mine at the age of thirteen. At sixteen I was an official in my local union.

"I quit the coal mine and started working in steel in Cambridge, Ohio, in 1909. I was then twenty-one. I stayed in Cambridge until

1914, when I moved to Warren, Ohio, and became a member of the Amalgamated Association of Iron, Steel, and Tin Workers. I served as president of three steel lodges, as they were called, of the Amalgamated, and served two terms as president of the Trumbull County Trades Council, AF of L. I was a delegate to two national conventions of the Amalgamated and to five conventions of the Ohio State Federation of Labor.

"I moved to Birmingham in March, 1926. There was no labor movement worthy of the name in the steel industry at that time; consequently no union whatever existed in the Tennessee Coal, Iron, and Railroad Company in the Birmingham District."

Impetus was given union organization by the passage of the National Industrial Recovery Act of 1933 with its Section 7-A providing that employees "shall have the right to organize and bargain collectively through representatives of their own choosing." Having nothing to turn to in the way of real collective bargaining the men seized upon the "Employee Representation Plan" offered them by the employers. The unions hoped that they could use this plan as a means of turning the workers' minds to genuine collective bargaining. Indeed, they felt that there was a mandate from the New Deal for them to utilize this means of building unions. But the promise of help in bringing about genuine collective bargaining through the company unions was a vain shadow. The big corporations, including the Tennessee Coal and Iron Company, moved in adroitly and began to capture this opportunity to plant company unions among their employees.

Mr. Crawford says, "The company imposed the company unions —called the Employees Representation Plan—on the workers. No one was asked to sign anything expressing approval. No officers were elected, no meetings of workers were held, no dues were collected. All that the workers were asked to do was to vote for representatives once a year. After the election the workers had absolutely no control over the representatives.

"I was appointed by the old Amalgamated Association of Iron, Steel, and Tin Workers as the first labor organizer ever to attempt the unionization of the steelworkers employed by the TCI. I did my job as a roller in the sheet mill and gave all of my spare time to building the AF of L Union—the Amalgamated—which fought the company union vigorously.

"About this time the Steel Code hearing was held in Washington by officials of the NRA. I was asked by the workers of the sheet mill to go to Washington and tell the story of the southern steel workers. A collection was made in the mill to pay my expenses.

"Although I had been granted a leave of absence, when the company learned my business in Washington two foremen were sent after me into downtown Birmingham, approximately twelve miles from the plant, to inform me that my leave of absence had been cancelled and I had to report back on the job. I informed the foremen that these workers had confidence in me, had raised the money to send me on the trip, and they could tell management I would see them when I returned from Washington.

"At the close of the hearings in Washington, after I had made my statement before the committee, President Green requested the administrator, Hugh Johnson, to protect me on my job since I had been threatened with discharge for making the trip to Washington. I was never fired.

"Upon my return, the union sponsored a mass meeting in Ensley City Park, where a crowd estimated at from five to seven thousand gathered to hear my report on the trip. For the first time in the history of Birmingham, a man speaking to labor had before him both the white and colored workers employed in TCI."

Thanks to Bill Crawford's persistence and courage other meetings sponsored by the union and attended by whites and Negroes were held.

"Not long after that the company union was declared illegal and ordered dissolved because 'it was imposed on the workers rather than chosen by them.' There was consternation among the corporations because of the sudden death of the company unions. The ruling was that meetings could no longer be held by company unions on company property. Forced out into the sunlight the company unions died.

"The TCI hastily called the company union representatives together and they drew up a new company union plan. The workers were asked to vote in favor of the new plan or the old plan, leaving no choice but to vote for a continuation of the company union. The Amalgamated called a mass meeting a day or two later to expose the trick. The company countered by changing the election date to the day before the union's mass meeting.

"I was working on the midnight turn when a number of our active people talked the situation over with me. It really appeared hopeless. There was apparently no way for us to advise the union people not to vote in this phoney election the company was holding. Suddenly one of the fellows said, 'if we only had an airplane to fly over these plants and throw out handbills telling the workers of the trick being pulled, we would have a chance to give the people the facts.'

"I immediately grabbed this idea, went into Birmingham, hired an airplane, got my printing done, and at the change of shift at 3 P.M. that day I flew over the plants at Ensley, Fairfield, and Bessemer throwing out leaflets asking the workers to refuse to vote.

"That was my first airplane ride. The trip was made in a small two passenger plane. The air was rough and the ride was extremely uncomfortable, and being my first ride it was a brand new experience. I was glad to get on the ground again!

"The election was a complete flop. However, the company claimed that eight-six per cent of those who participated in the election voted in favor of the new plan so the company union still survived for a period."

When the CIO came into being, a number of good scrapping union men swung into line behind it. Bill Crawford was in the forefront in this group.

"In August, 1941," his story continues, "I went on the steel union staff, and in May, 1942, at the first constitutional convention of the United Steelworkers, I was elected director of District 35 and still hold that elective office. I was president of the Birmingham Industrial Union Council from May, 1937, to April, 1942, when my office and home were moved to Atlanta. My territory covers Georgia, North and South Carolina, Tennessee, Virginia, and part of southern Kentucky."

When the master agreement between the United States Steel Corporation and the United Steelworkers of America was signed, it became operative in the plants of the TCI. Since then the steel workers in Birmingham have shared in the many benefits won through the negotiations of company and management.

In the eleven years Mr. Crawford has lived in Atlanta he has won the confidence of his fellow citizens. Among his offices, he is a member of the Board of Trustees, Greater Atlanta Community Chest; vice-president, Atlanta School of Social Work; and on the board of the Atlanta Urban League.

In October, 1951, C. H. Gillman declined to run again for the office of president of the Georgia State Industrial Union Council. Mr. Crawford was elected to the presidency of the Council, and continues his full-time job of director of Steelworkers, District 35.

One of Mr. Crawford's satisfactions is that young Bill is a member of the CIO staff in the South.

When Carey Haigler, CIO Alabama state director, learned that this book was being written he said he would like to pay a tribute in it to his old friend Bill Crawford. I quote a few paragraphs from this appreciation:

> The part played by Bill Crawford in organizing the steel industry in Alabama and the South can hardly be over-stated. He had worked in the coal mines and steel plants in his home state, Ohio, and was one of the few men in Alabama familiar with the old AF of L Amalgamated Association of Iron, Steel, and Tin Workers. He became one of the first, if not the first man to sign a card in the Steel Workers Organizing Committee, which commenced its campaign in the late thirties.
>
> Bill went on a number of dangerous missions during his work in Alabama. He was in and out of Gadsden often—the toughest town in the CIO organizing campaign. Owing to his frank and honest efforts to work for the organization of working men into real collective bargaining unions, and also his outstanding activities in behalf of justice

to Negro as well as white workers, every sort of pressure possible and every lie cunning minds could concoct were used against Bill Crawford, but he continued to lead in the union movement.

Along with Rube Farr, the late John Lewis, and the late D. L. Huey, I believe most of the credit for the establishment of unions in the Tennessee Coal and Iron Company belongs to Bill Crawford.

Charles Mathias

Charles Mathias is the kind of vital, intense young union leader who always turns a straight chair around and sits backwards in it, resting his arms on the support. This is the high sign that here is a man who is ready to spend the rest of the evening, if necessary, in working out the solution to whatever problem the organization may face.

Charlie spends about eighteen nights out of every month in such meetings and conferences, in addition to his everyday activities with the United Steelworkers of America and with the CIO Atlanta Industrial Union Council. He has headed the Council for four consecutive terms, making it an integrated part of the community in which it exists.

When Charlie comes into the room, you know that the talk will be stirring and provocative. I use those two words because they happen to be favorites of his—and they serve as a capsule description of his personality. With his deep blue eyes and wavy black hair, he is a stimulating person possessed of seemingly endless vitality.

Charlie was born in Baltimore County, Maryland. He was of the generation that first began to earn its own living in the year 1930. It was not an auspicious moment to start a career, but he not only served an apprenticeship as an armature winder but put in four years of night school at Maryland Institute and at Baltimore Tech.

It was in 1935 that he learned the lesson which has governed his life since that time. He had gone to work for the Gold Dust Corporation (now Lever Brothers) as an electrician. The plant was not organized. The working force had the poor morale which is natural under conditions where job security is non-existent, and seniority a matter of "guess and wonder." There was only one solution to the problem: organization. Charlie became a dues-paying member of the AF of L Soap & Glycerine Workers, threw himself into the struggle to unite his fellow employees, and found himself their elected leader, at the age of twenty-two, when the plant was successfully organized.

Results in the plant spoke for themselves—and another devoted unionist had been born.

Now, let Charlie tell the rest of his story. It begins two years later:

"Big things were just beginning to happen when I went to work for Bethlehem Steel. My job was as electrician in the coke ovens department of Bethlehem's Sparrows Point plant.

"This was in the middle of that historic time when the SWOC-CIO was engaged in its tremendous job of setting up one industrial union for the whole steel industry. The newspapers were full of it. Everybody from the President of the United States to the head of the NAM had something to say about it. College professors were coining new terms to describe it. They called it 'one of the most significant sociological developments of the twentieth century'—and some of them called it 'the last step on the road to hell.' Out at the plant, we didn't have much time to worry about what was said, or what the college professors called it. We had work to do, and it was time to do it.

"It was a while later that the CIO opened its drive in the South, but I think it is interesting to note that four of the leading figures in the Bethlehem organizing campaign have been or are now leaders in the South. Topmost was courageous Van A. Bittner, who died with his boots on in 1949. There were also John V. Riffe, formerly Van's good right arm, and now CIO southern director; Lorne Nelles, present assistant to John Riffe, and John Ramsay, director of community relations for the southern drive.

"It was a stirring and provocative job to organize Bethlehem Steel. It took almost five years to overcome the legal—and illegal—obstacles that were placed in the path of SWOC, but the all-important

NLRB election was won in September, 1941. In the intervening years, I had served as shop steward and chairman of the coke ovens department, recording secretary of the SWOC local 1224 (now USA locals 2609 and 2610), delegate to the union's 1940 Conference in Chicago, and division chairman and grievance chairman in the coke ovens, blast furnaces, gas engine department, and electrical repair shop.

"Then, in 1942, I took employment with the Atlantic Steel Company in Atlanta, Georgia. After several months of active membership in the Steelworkers local, serving on the plant grievance and bargaining committee, I took my first full-time union job with the Textile Workers, who needed a man for Georgia director. Shortly thereafter, I went on the International staff of the CIO Ship Yard Workers as an organizer for South Georgia and Florida. In 1943, I settled down for a while to service the local at the Merrill Stevens Yard in Jacksonville, after we won our NLRB election and negotiated the local's first contract. Just a few months before I went into the army, I was assigned to the Chattanooga, Tennessee, area of the Steelworkers.

"They say that the army 'separates the men from the boys.' I don't know that it's a lot different in the labor movement. Different as the two are in fact, the basic psychology is the same. Either you shoulder your responsibilities for yourself and your fellow human beings, or you take the short, selfish view and protect your own hide. You find both kinds of folks in both places.

"After fourteen months in northern France and Central Europe, where I saw 158 days of combat duty and won two battle stars, I came back to Atlanta to go to work for W. H. Crawford, director USA District 35, exactly a week before the 1946 steel strike. I was assigned to do service and administrative work for all steel locals in the Atlanta area. You might call that 'out of the frying pan into the fire,' but that's where I've been ever since—and where I'd be honored to stay—in the struggle for the equal rights and opportunities of all my fellow Americans.

"I'd like to point out just one way in which the Steelworkers have acted to carry out that philosophy. In 1949, the workers in Atlantic Steel Company were forced on strike after bargaining at the table failed to gain a much-needed insurance and pension program. While we were on the bricks, the national union set a pension pattern with Bethlehem Steel which compelled Atlantic to come across with an offer.

"What they offered was a hundred dollar a month minimum pension for white employees with twenty-five years service, and eighty dollars for Negro employees with the same service. It was one of the happiest moments in my life when the local union members right here in Atlanta, Georgia, refused to accept such a discriminatory offer. They turned it down flatly, and in the end, we won a hundred dollars for everybody. That, to me, is democracy in action.

"Another victory we are proud of involves a legal battle that went on for years and years. When the NLRB election was won by the union at Atlantic in 1941, a stenographic error was made in the filing of the official form, which resulted in the certification of the local, rather than both the local and the national union of which it was a part. This meant that the union's district director and international representatives were excluded from full participation in bargaining.

"The company used every legal device in the book to keep the error from being corrected. Attorneys were used by the carload to prevent the NLRB from recognizing the error. Finally, in 1950—nearly ten years later—the union maneuvered a plant election to determine the issue. Did the workers really want the national union to make bargaining decisions for them? (The company naturally tried to insinuate that such an idea was outlandish.) The election resulted in a tremendous victory for the union by a margin of twelve to one. So, after years of legal tightrope walking, the company was forced to admit the mistake."

That's the end of Charlie's story, but I can't let it end without a final comment. As a Catholic, the father of two children, he takes his place in his community and church life as an individual. And as president of the Atlanta Industrial Union Council, he carries his union into the community. His firm belief in political action has resulted in a burst of enthusiasm among his associates; and his interest in the community has been recently exemplified by his part in developing and carrying through the highly succesful Regional Community Services Institute in Atlanta. At this moment, radio and newspaper tell me that our friend Charlie Mathias has been made chairman of the Fulton County Board of Public Welfare, of which he has long been a useful member.

Carey Haigler

The report of the Twelfth Constitutional Convention of the Alabama and Bessemer Industrial Union Councils, which was quoted at length in the chapter on "The Movement," gives an encouraging account of the organizing activities of CIO unions in Alabama. Carey E. Haigler, CIO state director of Alabama since 1946, had an important part in that story.

Like most of the CIO directors in the South, Mr. Haigler is southern. He was born in what is now known as Ensley, on the outskirts of Birmingham, August 9, 1902. He is a tall, large-framed man, blue-eyed and blond, with quiet manners and a reluctance to talk about himself. He is a member of the Martin Memorial Methodist Church, and also a member of the Church Board of Stewards. Mr. Haigler's story follows:

"My first real job was in a steel plant, commencing in Ensley. After being employed in several departments at the Tennessee Coal and Iron Company, and in Republic Steel, I joined the old Amalgamated Association of Iron, Steel, and Tin Workers in Fairfield, near Birmingham, in 1933. This was three years before the CIO came. Almost immediately I had an unhappy experience. I was elected president of what is now Steelworkers Local Union 1131 on Sunday afternoon, and was discharged by the company on the following day. This was back in 1934, at a time when there was no National Labor Relations Board to which I might appeal."

(W. H. Crawford has told me that Carey was offered his job back in the steel mill if he would repudiate the union and give the company union the credit for getting him back to work. This he flatly refused to do, saying "I'll crawl out of Alabama on my hands and knees before I will take the job and give the company union the credit for it.")

"After hanging around in a practically unemployed capacity for about eighteen months, I managed to get a job with the Soil Conservation Service, U. S. Department of Agriculture, and was employed there for about six years.

"Then I went to work as field representative of the United Steelworkers in Birmingham in February, 1942. When the United Mine Workers withdrew from the CIO in 1942, I was appointed assistant regional director of CIO, and secretary-treasurer of the Alabama CIO Council.

"Almost immediately after my appointment as field representative of the United Steelworkers of America, I inherited some tough assignments. At the Holt, Alabama Blast Furnaces leased by TCI and R. R. Company, I assisted in a small way in winning the first NLRB-conducted election in that company's plants. This was probably one of the first elections in U. S. Steel's mills. Newly elected director, R. E. Farr, of District 36 United Steelworkers was a tower of strength at Holt. He also played an important role in the campaign at Republic Steel.

"A short time later we won bargaining rights in the Birmingham Thomas Plant of Republic Steel. This was close and determined by a check of membership cards against the company's payroll. Once again I was present at the winning count.

"For a short time I assisted Tim Flynn in the highly successful campaign at TCI's main plants in the Birmingham District.

"In mid-summer of 1942, I was notified by Alabama Regional Director Beddow that I was being assigned to Gadsden and that our main objective was the organization of Republic Steel in that city. Goodyear Tire and Rubber Company and the plant of the Dwight Manufacturing Company were also on the agenda.

"Reluctantly I journeyed to Gadsden with the feeling that it could possibly be my last earthly undertaking, for Gadsden was considered to be a tough anti-CIO town. After a sensational mob action that saw President Sherman Dalrymple of the Rubber Workers beaten almost to death on the courthouse steps in downtown Gadsden, union representatives led a rather precarious existence in that district. John House, a representative of the United Rubber Workers, had been beaten severely in September of 1941. William Dunn of the Steelworkers had been shot at, and Will Watts, also of the Steelworkers, had been threatened on several occasions and jailed once or twice on trumped up charges.

"Morton Elder of the Steelworkers was my predecessor in Gadsden and had built some semblance of organization under trying circumstances. Despite this, after winning a strike and an NLRB election at the Birmingham Slag Company plant in September, 1941, there was not a single collective bargaining agreement between any CIO affiliate and any company in the Gadsden area at the time of my assignment.

"After getting acquainted with my task I found Louise D. Yates working part-time for the Steelworkers. William W. Cherry, A. C. Burttram, and Robert McGruder, along with myself, were the staff. We met with some immediate success and found about four hundred union men ready and determined to organize CIO unions in Gadsden.

"Another thing that helped a great deal was a change in attitude toward CIO on the part of Mayor J. Herbert Meighan. Mr. Meighan had been angered by repeated efforts on the part of some of the industrialists to usurp his authority as mayor of Gadsden. At a readily granted interview he told me that he would be impartially fair to both sides and that promise was kept one hundred per cent.

"The success at Republic caused the Textile Workers Union to send Helen Gregory, Ted Thomas, 'Pat' (Margaret) Knight, and Elmer Daugherty to Gadsden, and a successful campaign was inaugurated at Dwight Manufacturing Company. Pressure from workers at the Goodyear plant caused the Rubber Workers to send 'Jimmie' Jones to Gadsden for a fast and furious campaign that also proved highly successful.

"I was appointed to the U. S. Steel Wage Rate Commission and left town before any success was attained. The real credit goes to those mentioned above and the many good, tried, and true union members in Gadsden and Etowah County who, after all, made the real sacrifice."

During the turbulent years of organizing in Gadsden I was in the city several times, but never at the time of violence. I saw John House a few days after he was almost killed by the group of men who went to his office, slugged him on the head, and left him lying in a pool of blood. He told me that he had never seen any of his attackers, and thought they were brought in from outside to do away with him.

As the unions gained in strength, public opinion softened toward them. Then came the signing of agreements between the large steel and rubber companies and the national unions, of which Carey Haigler has spoken. There were still rough spots, but management and labor relations steadily improved.

In the spring of 1946 a notable occasion took place in Gadsden. The United Rubber Workers, then under contract with the Goodyear Company, celebrated the third anniversary of securing bargaining rights by giving a banquet to representatives and officers of other unions, and officials of the Republic Steel Company, Goodyear Rubber, and the Dwight Manufacturing Company (textiles). Community leaders were also invited.

From all reports, that was a happy occasion and everyone seems to have congratulated everyone else. Gadsden is conspicuous among a number of cities which have had to pass through a period of battle wherein industrialists tried to beat down unions by violence, but finding that this would not pay, finally emerged into sane management-labor relations through collective bargaining agreements. After that came the steady process of replacing battle with peace, law, and order.

At the time of the celebration Allan Swim was publicity director of the CIO Organizing Committee. His curiosity was aroused and he spent several days in Gadsden seeing representative people in civic, fraternal, business, trade, and church groups. The consensus was that the higher wages flowing from the union agreements meant millions of new money to Gadsden every year. The economic life-blood of the whole city and its surrounding area was stimulated by this increased purchasing power.

Marked also was the appreciation of a new status for union people because of their interest in the total welfare of the city. These men and women through their union meetings learned more than ever before of the needs of their community, and the part they could take in making it a better place in which to live. Some of them were elected to the city council, while other union members served on city and social welfare boards. Some of the ministers testified that instead of the unions taking people away from the churches, they were making it more possible for working people to attend church and contribute to its support—better wages did that.

PAUL CHRISTOPHER, AN "OLD" YOUNG FRIEND

The first young friend I made in the 1937 southern drive of the CIO was Paul R. Christopher of South Carolina. We met in Steve Nance's office in Atlanta, for Paul was then with the Textile Workers Union. Our friendship has deepened through the years and I have worked with him in many places. I am glad this book gives me opportunity to pay him tribute.

After the election of Estes Kefauver to the U. S. Senate in 1948, the *Knoxville Journal,* speaking editorially, declared that the people of Tennessee had swapped Ed Crump for Paul Christopher as their political dictator. Though this is a false statement, it reflects the truth of CIO's growth among Tennessee's industrial workers and its members' increasing political awareness during the eight years Paul had then served as CIO director in the "Volunteer State."

The editorial also, unconsciously, pays tribute to Christopher's ability and astuteness in drawing together opposing forces in a common and good cause. Undoubtedly, Paul Christopher had been the most powerful single force in bringing Tennessee's industrial unions to their considerable proportions, thereby increasing their political importance.

Christopher was born in the little town of Easley, South Carolina, Pickens County, in a mill house owned by Alice Mill, on February 14, 1910, of parents who were textile workers. His mother worked six months learning to weave in Alice Mill before she drew her first pay, as was the custom in those days. She had to go to work before the Alice Mill management would permit Paul's father and mother to live in a company house. His father was a loom fixer.

The family moved to Greenville, S. C., and Paul went to work in a mill there at the age of fourteen. He early became active in union affairs and proved to be a natural and able leader. Two years spent in studying textile engineering at Clemson College made Paul especially useful to the union.

Now forty-one years old, Christopher has shown judgment and versatility in meeting many tough propositions. Indeed, he goes out of his way to meet a particular challenge. He resigned his position as South Carolina director of the Textile Workers Union in 1940, and went to Tennessee as CIO director on the staff of Allan S. Haywood, director of organization in the national CIO. I am told that CIO's membership in Tennessee then was probably less than 12,000, including some 7000 coal miners, who were later lost when John L. Lewis took the Mine Workers out of CIO in 1942. Mr. Crump was shouting loudly that CIO would not be permitted to organize in Memphis. The American Newspaper Guild, nevertheless held its annual convention there in 1940.

With the special blessing of Allan S. Haywood, Paul went to work to mobilize organizing forces made available through several CIO international unions, thus adding many union representatives to the drive to organize thousands of unorganized industrial workers in Memphis and in other parts of Tennessee.

Industrial and political leaders in Roan County had said no CIO union would be allowed to organize in Rockwood or Harriman. Organizers had been beaten, kidnapped, and shot. In September, 1941, two CIO men were waylaid and nearly beaten to death. CIO forces were marshaled to complete the campaigns at a paper mill in

Harriman and the iron smelter at Rockwood. These beatings were
avenged by successful organization at both places. Paul was in
charge there.

The huge K-25 atomic installation at Oak Ridge was organized in
the first major Tennessee campaign following the creation of CIO's
Southern Organizing Committee in 1946. The Aluminum Company
of America at Alcoa, with over 7000 employees (11,000 during
World War II), was organized first by the Aluminum Workers, but
in 1944 voted to affiliate with the United Steelworkers. Alcoa is now
almost solidly organized.

Mr. Christopher attributes CIO's success in Tennessee to the able
leaders who have been developed throughout the state, and others
who have been assigned to that state by national unions.

Paul and his staff are persistent. They never give up. Witness the
victory at the Bemis Cotton Mill on the fifth election. There are
numbers of other places where three and four organizing drives and
elections were required before CIO unions won bargaining rights.

There are good reasons CIO as an organization and its nearly
100,000 members and leaders are respected in Tennessee. One of
those reasons is Paul Revere Christopher.

Grover Hathaway, Meatpackers' Man

Grover Hathaway's story which follows makes an introduction
hardly necessary. He is one of the small group of men who woke up
to the need for unions early in his career and cast his lot with the
labor movement.

I remember him in my early years in Georgia as he helped build
unions wherever and whenever he had a chance. Whether it was
steelworkers in the Southern Spring Bed Company or quarry workers or others, Mr. Hathaway put his hand to the task. His long, hard,
untiring efforts in organizing meatpackers in the southern states is
his most notable achievement. He has been cooperative with CIO
unions as a whole and helped in the formative days and later in the
making of the Atlanta Industrial Union Council and the State
Council.

"I was born in the state of North Carolina on February 5, 1908, the son of Willie Dale and Alice Lee Hathaway. My father was a cabinetmaker by trade. My mother died when I was nine years old. When I was twelve years old my father married again, and at the age of fourteen I quit school in the ninth grade and started to work for myself.

"That same year my father, step-mother, a half-brother and two half-sisters, and my own sister moved to Atlanta, Georgia, leaving me and my kid brother in Wilson, North Carolina, where I boarded and worked. At the age of fifteen, lured by glowing reports from my father of the opportunities in Atlanta, and having naturally itchy feet, I gave up my job and came to Atlanta. There I went to work for my father who was foreman on a construction job and whose father-in-law was superintendent on the same job.

"I think it is safe to say that it was between the ages of fifteen and seventeen that I first began to acquire a curiosity concerning the discrimination between the races. Prior to this time, I had always accepted the fact that the Negro race was a different race of people, and true to my environment I held a sort of contempt for any race other than the gentile. However, soon after I began working on the construction job in Atlanta I learned that the real earnings were in the skilled trades. I also learned that while, when I asked questions of the white skilled tradesmen I got a short answer and sometimes no answer at all, for the most part the Negro tradesmen would take time to answer the questions I continuously had at the tip of my tongue and would upon request—and many times without having to be requested—show me how to perform the operations which they performed so proficiently.

"It was some time before I became aware of the fact that while the Negro common laborers and the Negro professional tradesmen, such as brickmasons, carpenters, and so forth, worked side by side with the whites, often doing the same work, at the same time there was a distinct difference in pay. My own sense of fair play rebelled at this and it wasn't long before this same sense of fair play was brought into active operation.

"I recall vividly one labor foreman on the job, a big, burly, red-faced man, full of oaths and profanity, who was constantly adjuring workers to move faster, get on the ball, because a one-armed man across the street wants your job if you can't do it. He was particularly vicious to the Negro workers, constantly threatening bodily harm and pulling rude and uncouth practical jokes on them. He drank almost constantly, despite the fact that this was the era of prohibition, at least in the state of Georgia.

"The incident that really opened my eyes to discrimination occurred on a hot, sultry afternoon—a day on which this foreman had been particularly vicious to everyone with whom he had come in contact. Half-drunk on the job, he came staggering down one of the gangways toward a Negro laborer who was pushing a wheelbarrow full of mortar which required all his strength and which allowed him no opportunity to maneuver out of the way. The foreman lurched into the workman and in his half-drunk condition fell over into the wheelbarrow with his face and shoulders completely mired in mortar. You can readily realize that he was a considerable spectacle, as he rose dripping with mortar and bellowing profane oaths, pawing at his eyes and face to get the mortar off.

"It was out of a sort of horror that I watched him as he reached down and picked up a piece of 2 by 4 and charged on the helpless Negro worker. I recall vividly to this day the look of anguish upon the face of the Negro as the 2 by 4 wielded by the burly foreman landed its first blow across his shoulders. The foreman beat the Negro to his knees with the heavy bludgeon, all the time giving vent to oaths and profanity, accusing the Negro of deliberately tripping him, while the Negro gave further anguished wails of pain and protested his innocence.

"I stood and watched the foreman rain several blows upon the man's head and shoulders until he was knocked unconscious and lay prostrate at the feet of the foreman. At that time the foreman threw away the 2 by 4 and began kicking the prostrate Negro in the side and the groins.

"I stood there waiting for some of the other Negroes or some other white workers on the job to rush forward and drag the foreman away. But not a soul seemed to stir. Soon I could stand it no longer and, inasmuch as I was standing amidst a pile of bricks about fifteen feet away, I heaved a brick at the foreman, catching him in the back of the head and laying him out cold. There they lay—the Negro whom the foreman had beaten and kicked unconscious and the foreman whom I had knocked unconscious with the brick.

"Of course, there was an immediate uproar and consternation, because I did not stop at throwing one brick. I threw several more at the foreman as he lay there, giving full vent to my wrath until another workman caught me by the arms and held me.

"An ambulance was called. Typical of the discrimination at work, an ambulance representing a white service was first to arrive. Although both men lay there, this ambulance driver would not take the Negro to the municipal hospital despite the fact that this same hospital took care of both white and Negro patients in different sections.

"This was one time when it was of great benefit to me that I was the son of another foreman and the step-grandson of the superintendent of the job.

"Later I was to have some of the white workers come to me sheepishly and admit they thought that I had done right in attacking the foreman. Needless to say from that time on I was received as a friend by the Negro people; and when later I was assigned to work as a brickmason, my father took me to one elderly Negro craftsman and asked him if he would teach me how to lay brick. This Negro, who is now dead and gone, could neither read nor write, nor could he belong to a labor union. But he was recognized as a master in his trade. I give full credit to this Negro brickmason for teaching me, to the extent that later I had no trouble in getting myself apprenticed and becoming a member of the brickmasons local of the AF of L. There, however, I suffered from the antiquated regulations of the Brickmasons Union, which held rigidly to the premise that an apprentice was not a brickmason—at least until he had served three years' apprenticeship. These same union members thought nothing of demanding that I do a full day's work, on jobs requiring the technical skill of a full mason, within a year after I began serving my apprenticeship. Needless to say the apprentice pay was considerably below the full-scale rate.

"At the age of seventeen I married, and within a few months, like thousands of others, was lured to Florida by the promise of full work at exceptionally good wages. There I worked for less than one month before I fell off a double scaffold and fractured several vertebrae in my back. I was advised by the physician that once out of the hospital I would never be able to do any work which required the constant bending and phyiscal labor of professional brickmasons. I found the doctors were right. As a result I was forced to accept other work. Among the many jobs I held was that of a taxicab driver.

"I was discharged twice from the Yellow Cab Company because of my attempts to organize the drivers into a union. Later the Yellow Cab Company and the Black & White Cab Company of Atlanta were amalgamated and again attempts were made to organize the drivers into a union. This time the effort was successful. Due to the fact that I had accepted another job some two months before the completion of the union, I was not a member at the time the organization was granted a charter and negotiated the first contract. However, the group of drivers, in appreciation of the work I had done while working with them, granted me an honorary membership in the local union.

"My next contact with unions as such was in 1935, while I was working at the Southern Spring Bed Company. This was during the era of the NRA. The Upholsterers' Union of the AF of L made attempts to organize the workers of the Southern Spring Bed Company. Like many others, I joined the union, attended several meetings, and heard a number of speeches. But immediately the NRA was declared illegal the representative of the Upholsterers' Union disappeared from the scene and nobody could find where he had gone.

"It was in 1937 that one B. T. Judd, a field representative of the Steel Workers Organizing Committee came to Atlanta and began organizational attempts. This was during the period when the UAW members of what is now Local 34, the Atlanta Chevrolet Plant, had begun to play their part in the then young CIO labor movement. B. T. Judd had contacted a number of people in the Southern Spring Bed Company and called a meeting. On the same evening, he had called a meeting for the General Shoe Company workers. That afternoon B. T. Judd was beaten by thugs employed by the General Shoe Company, and he appeared at the meeting that evening with his head almost completely swathed in bandages.

"I arrived at the meeting somewhat late. Although the hall held nearly three hundred fifty people, I was unable to get a seat. Along with many other workers of the Southern Spring Bed Company, I sat on the edge of the platform from which B. T. Judd was speaking.

"Judd thought he was speaking to a large group of the General Shoe Company workers. It was only when he asked for a check of the group in the house that he was astounded to find there were less than fifty people at the meeting from the General Shoe Company, while there were more than three hundred there from the Southern Spring Bed Company.

"After talking for some time Judd invited the workers from either plant to make comments upon his statement of CIO policies and principles and to state their own feelings with regard to organizing. As I sat there rubbing my hands together, looking at the large callouses and blisters which kept them always sore—so sore sometimes that my wife had to assist me in getting my clothes on in the morning—I thought of the miserably poor wages which we were being paid and the conditions under which we worked in the plant. And I envisioned this same job working under decent conditions and earning wages which would enable me to move out of my two-room upstairs apartment into a house with a yard in which my children could play.

"Looking around, waiting for someone else to take the responsibility of speaking first, I seemed to hear only intense silence. I could stand it no longer. I rose to my feet. I held my hands out in front of me and I called the attention of the workers of the Southern

Spring Bed Company to them, and called upon them to look at their own hands and think of the conditions which prevailed at the plant in which we worked. Not being used to public speaking at that time, I am quite sure that my speech was crude and sometimes incoherent. Nevertheless there were just a few minutes before the workers were shouting in unison with me. My talk seemed to have broken the ice and we were there for at least another two hours. It seemed that everybody wanted to talk at once.

"A meeting was agreed upon, to be held the following week. As we left the hall, B. T. Judd ranged up alongside me and said, 'Boy, you are going to be president of this local union and if you keep on like you were going tonight you are going somewhere in the labor movement.' Little did I know how prophetic his words were to be.

"At the next meeting of the group I was elected president and a committee was formed to contact the management of the Southern Spring Bed Company to present our demands for recognition.

"It was with some trepidation the following morning that I led the committee into the office of the superintendent, who greeted us with a rather surly growl and inquired the nature of our business. When informed of our reasons for being there, he threw one of the tantrums for which he was famous, ordered us out of his office and threatened that if we did not go quickly enough he would kick us out. As a result of this reception we held another meeting later that week. We took a strike vote and came to the conclusion that, at the appointed date and time, the committee would again contact the local management, and if the reception was similar to the previous one we would advise the management that we were going on strike.

"We met with management and our reception was different only to the extent the superintendent was even more vicious than before. When we advised him that as the result of his denial and action we would be forced to call the workers out on strike, he assured us in his own inimitable language that he would see us in Hades, and that if we went on strike every man who went out would lose his job. Needless to say we struck and for five weeks the company, aided and abetted by hired thugs, the entire Atlanta police department, the sheriff and his deputies, pulled every trick known to the Mohawk Valley formula, and in our opinion initiated some additional ones.

"After the period of five weeks the company, recognizing that all its efforts were in vain, agreed to sit down and negotiate. Although ours was a tremendous victory, everyone was so tired that it was difficult to realize our success. After some two days of further nego- tiations, a contract was agreed upon and the majority of workers returned to work.

"As a result of the compromise agreement almost one hundred members who had been replaced by scabs while the strike was on were left out of a job. I still think of the Southern Spring Bed Com- pany workers as one of the finest group of loyal trade union people I have ever known. For, upon returning to work, those who were employed every week for a year reported—just as regularly as the paydays came—to the union committee and donated a portion of their earnings to support those workers who had not returned to work, and their families.

"Within less than one year's time we were able to bring ninety- eight of the hundred workers who were out back on their jobs, and had an offer to the other two of their jobs, but they chose not to return to work because they had found jobs they liked better. I still think of the return of the ninety-eight members as an even greater victory than the strike itself.

"I was president of Local 1970 of the Southern Spring Bed Com- pany from 1937 through 1940. Our local union was the second CIO local to be established in the state of Georgia. Needless to say I became an active worker in the organizing activities of CIO in the city of Atlanta and the state of Georgia. I was eventually employed as a part-time organizer for the Steel Workers Organizing Commit- tee. I also served as a part-time organizer for the Quarry Workers International Union of North America which is now the United Stone and Allied Products Workers of America.

"In 1940 I was offered a job on the staff of the PWOC, or Pack- inghouse Workers Organizing Committee, which I accepted in May, 1940. It was a privilege in 1943 to assist in setting up the constitutional convention for what is now the United Packinghouse Workers of America, CIO.

"When I came on the staff of PWOC in 1940 we had less than three hundred members, all of whom were in three plants in Birmingham, Alabama. I have seen the district now known as District 9 of the United Packinghouse Workers of America grow from that size to a district representing between five thousand and seven thousand dues-paying members, covering at this writing seventy-five plants and thirty-five local unions. And even now, after a little over ten years, I feel that we have only scratched the surface of the potential organizing possibilities in this district. I have seen our international union grow from a few scattered thousands to a membership of approximately two hundred thousand members. The UPWA is now rated among the ten major international unions within the CIO.

"In 1948 the United Packinghouse Workers of America undertook to lick the Big Four packers alone, having been double-crossed by the Amalgamated Meatcutters Union, AF of L. Although we were not successful in getting the wage increase for which we had gone on strike, we did weld ourselves into a union which, because of our policies and principles, we believe, is second to none in solidarity and the ability to work together within the ranks of CIO international unions.

"It has been my privilege to go into cities and towns in the southern states and establish local unions in areas which had never before seen an active union. It has been my pleasure to help the workers negotiate contracts which in turn have resulted in making it possible for those same workers, who once went to work afoot or on bicycles, to ride to work in good used or new automobiles. I have seen them leave hovels in which they at one time were forced to live and move into decent houses. I have seen them change from tired, careworn workers with a lack of lustre in their eyes to trim, energetic persons whose health was so much better because contract conditions enabled them to take care of themselves and their families adequately. I have seen old discrimination practices cast to the side, and workers

gather freely regardless of race, sex, color, or nationality to discuss
their problems within their plant and their union.

"When I compare this to the days of the early forties, when police
officers, deputy sheriffs, and such groups considered it an evening
sport to break up a union meeting simply because there were white
and Negro people gathering in the same hall, I feel that we have
come a long way.

"I have heard the plaintive cries of management as we forced
them to eliminate practices of discrimination and prejudice because
of race, sex, color, and creed. I have seen men killed and women
and children beaten because of their loyalty and devotion to principles of unionism.

"While I recognize that we have come a long way toward organizing labor, particularly in the South, we still have a long hard road
to go before we can consider that real progress has been made.
Nevertheless, as I look back upon those last ten years, I consider
every night that I lost sleep and every mile that I traveled worth
while. However, it is not our position to look backward. It is our
job to look forward, and to build and to build and to work until all
workers have become a part of this great labor movement."

ERNEST PUGH AND THE VIRGINIA TOUCH

In Virginia the sense of ancestry is so deep that even legislative
committees heckle witnesses as to their birthplace and residence.
This is particularly true in matters related to labor unions. I had
heard that my good friend, Ernest B. Pugh, CIO director of Virginia,
had had some funny experiences along these lines. So the next time
I saw him I asked about them. This is what he told me:

"I was one of the speakers at a legislative committee hearing in
Richmond, and observed that the first CIO speakers were challenged
as to their birthplace and residence. If they could not qualify as
Virginians, they were called 'foreigners' or 'Yankees.' Anticipating
this, when I was introduced as a speaker for a certain bill, I began
by saying:

"As ancestry seems to be important here I will briefly give mine and get that matter behind us so we can go on with the subject of this hearing. My forebears landed near Cape Henry, Virginia, Princess Anne County, in 1666. There were my great, great, great grandfather and his three brothers, John, Henry, and Peter, from Carnavonshire, Wales. All four of them came in 1666. I was born in Norfolk, within fifty miles of the original landing place of my forebears. I descended from that branch of the family headed by John.

"I have never attempted to count the generations since then, but it is a long time back, two hundred and eighty-five years ago, since that landing.

"One of the other brothers trekked into the Valley of Virginia. He now has descendants in Charlottesville and Waynesboro. I think this was Peter, who eventually located in Ohio. Some of his descendants became prominent in public affairs. Several were officers in the Confederate Army. Others were legislators and professional people.

"Gentlemen, just for the sake of the record, let it be noted that my ancestors landed on the shores of Virginia in 1666, and with that fact established, here is what I think of the piece of legislation now before you."

By this time I had gotten so interested in Mr. Pugh's ancestors that I asked more questions about his family. He said:

"The motto of the Pugh family in Gaelic means, 'Not physicians, but soul physicians.' In the personal application of this motto I like to feel that I am charged with a sympathetic sense of responsibility to listen to and alleviate the troubles, worries, and problems of my fellow men. I have found plenty of operation for this philosophy in the organized labor movement in the past half century. In 1900 I finished my apprenticeship as a machinist in Norfolk, at which time I was recording secretary of Machinists Local 11. Later I became president, and still later business agent for the International Association of Machinists for the territory of Norfolk, Portsmouth, and Newport News."

Mr. Pugh was in Chicago as CIO regional director when he was offered a job in the same capacity in his native state, and accepted.

On November 1, 1941, he came to the CIO director's office in Richmond.

Mr. Pugh has received the Selective Service Medal, presented by Congress and signed by the President, for meritorious service on the Board of Appeals. He was three times appointed by Governor Darden as delegate from Virginia to the National Conference on Labor Legislation, held annually in Washington.

In the seven years he has lived in Richmond, as CIO state director, Mr. Pugh has made scores of friends and shown a warm interest in the social progress of Richmond and of Virginia.

Among many organizations in which he has served are the Richmond Industrial Union Council, CIO; Virginia United Labor Committee, and Joint Labor Legislative Committee; Electoral Reform League; State Council for Training in Industry; Selective Service Appeals Board; Richmond War and Community Fund; Children's Home Society Board. He has also served as state management-labor consultant.

BERNARD BORAH

Bernard Borah was one of my special friends in the CIO. He was a fine young man, with a philosophical bent, which he gratified by getting a degree in psychology and philosophy while at the University of Tennessee. For about two years he was a research aide for the TVA, helping to conduct economic and sociological studies.

In his college years, Borah became keenly interested in the industrial union movement and did volunteer work for several CIO unions. From the summer of 1937 to that of 1942, Bernard was in turn a representative of the Amalgamated Clothing Workers of America and this union's southern director.

For a brief period he was with the National Council of Gas, Coke, and Chemical Workers, aiding in its formation. His union work was ended by enlistment in the army as a volunteer officer candidate. He came out of this training with a high record, and was until his death assistant civilian personnel officer, a task assigned him because of his experience with labor.

Bernard was a fine-looking man, well built and handsome, with black hair and dark eyes, and a direct look that quickly won confidence. His associates and union members always loved and trusted him. His sudden death under a thyroid operation in the New Mexico army camp where he was stationed was a shock to all who knew and loved him, and above all to his former union associates. We had kept up a correspondence during his army life, and he had written me a long and beautiful letter a week before he died. A friend who knew Borah has suggested that I give him the place that he has left absent by quoting from some of his letters.

The war situation has taken a slightly bad turn tonight. I've been sitting here listening to the radio. We were bound to have some setbacks, and it is just as well that the news comes now, to sober public opinion and make us buckle down. Too many people were about to get too lackadaisical about the war effort. . . .

Thank God for labor union experience. It teaches one patience, and the ability to accept setbacks without being greatly disturbed by them, knowing that diligence will bring eventual success. After all, working people always have more failures than successes, but like the traditional British, they always win the last battle.

And the war and the labor movement are alike in that: you must keep fighting, paying little attention to successes or failures along the road, keeping your equilibrium and your good sense and your passion for justice and your diligence, because after all the last battle and the whole war are the important things.

In the letter written a week before his death Bernard wrote:

The man who feels God in the universe and cannot explain Him or describe Him, but accepts Him without worrying about it . . . the man who realizes that if there is a heaven one can be sure of it only if we build with our own sweat and blood and brains on earth—the man who admires and loves goodness for itself alone, and who sees within man an ageless spirit, warm and good, seeking a good life—a man who loves man, and loves life, and loves justice—then to this man life becomes more important than death, and he must strive to do good and build goodness on earth.

HIGHLANDER FOLK SCHOOL

Recently I was at Highlander Folk School attending a meeting of the executive council of which I have been a member for many years. (Paul Christopher, Tennessee CIO director, is also a council member and devoted friend of the school.) As always when at this school I saw it as a seedbed of democracy and rejoiced that it had survived financial and other troubles to continue holding its light aloft there on the Cumberland Mountain top. Highlander's name has appeared several times in this book, and since it now appears again, I take this opportunity to refer to its interesting background.

Dr. Lillian Johnson of Memphis, well known educator, after retiring from her college teaching, moved to her modest summer place two miles from Monteagle, Tennessee, and made it her year-round residence. She developed the place as a community center for the mountain people of that neighborhood.

Myles Horton had spent some time studying in the Union Theological Seminary and found himself more and more wanting to apply his religion to improving conditions for industrial workers and farmers. In 1932 he heard that Dr. Johnson was going to retire from her community center work and might be interested in finding some one who would take over the program.

So Myles approached Dr. Johnson. She was interested and suggested that he take over the center for one year on a probationary basis. This he did and later enlarged the community center into Highlander Folk School. Several young men with high ideals assisted, but the two who remained for any length of time were Ralph Tefferteller, who was there for a considerable period, and Dr. James A. Dombrowski. Dr. Dombrowski had graduated from Union Theological Seminary and Emory University, before he joined the staff in 1932. He remained at Highlander ten or twelve years, until he took up other work.

The philosophy of the school can be judged by the following quotation, taken from the Highlander Statement of Purpose:

The times call for an affirmative program, based on a positive goal. An army of democracy deeply rooted in the lives, struggles, and traditions of the American people must be created. By broadening the scope of democracy to include everyone . . . the army of democracy would be so vast and determined that nothing undemocratic could stand in its path.

Highlander's program prepares men and women to take an active part in organizing and building strong, democratic unions. Students learn about making parliamentary procedure work. They learn about shop or grievance committees and how they can help solve problems that may become serious threats to good union-management relations if they are not settled. In addition, they get information about many other matters that stimulate their interest in the world at large. Industrial workers are learning at Highlander to appreciate the problems of farmers—while farmers are achieving a better understanding of labor unions. In race, in religious belief, in sectionalism, in world interest, southern men and women are learning to understand and like people, regardless of their backgrounds or differences.

Theory and practice are skilfully combined in workers' education in this union school. All over the South there are active, useful, union members applying what they have learned at Highlander. As one student wrote, summing up her experiences at the school:

"High on top of the Cumberland mountains in Tennessee, near the little village of Monteagle, lies the famous Highlander Folk School. . . . Everything at Highlander is high—its ideals, its standards, and its purpose. The school is an experience in real democracy. . . . It is Highlander's belief that democracy is not possible with only uncritical carrying out of orders from above, for there will be a common willingness to sacrifice only if there is a common confidence that the benefits of the future will be for all."

First sessions for industrial workers at Highlander began in the fall of 1932. These sessions lasted several weeks and were attended by both union and non-union workers, coal miners, occasional farmers, and unemployed men, some of whom later on came back as union members and leaders. As the program developed, recreational activities among the neighborhood people increased and the school became more and more of a community center.

Zylphia Horton, Myles' wife, has been of great assistance in the development of Highlander, and particularly invaluable as a leader of group singing. Mrs. Horton has worked with the public school, helping organize a parents' club, of which she is now president, to promote the school's welfare.

Mrs. Joanna Willimetz is in charge of the growing day nursery which has been an important factor in knitting Highlander into the lives of the people. "Joie," as she is appropriately nicknamed, is acting as executive of the school while Mr. Horton gives most of his time to directing the education program of the United Packinghouse Workers of America, CIO. The work with this progressive union is a new Highlander project, with all expenses carried by the union.

Emil Willimetz, husband of Joanna, operates the Film Service Center which serves unions and other groups with both picture stories and film strips. The Center has just completed a sound film strip, *Of a New Day Begun,* for the American Missionary Association's Race Relations Department at Fisk University. Sound scripts have also been completed for the CIO's Southern Organizing Committee and for another labor sponsor.

During my recent visit to Highlander I saw Stewart Meacham, one of the finest products of the church and the labor movement. I had heard of him in his work with the National Labor Relations Board, but had only met him twice before, and briefly. He and his wife, Charlotte, were at Highlander for three months as a preparation for going to India as missionaries of the Methodist Church to that nation's wretchedly poor and oppressed industrial workers.

Mr. Meacham has an excellent background for this enterprise. His father was a Presbyterian minister and the son started out on the same path, graduating from Union Theological Seminary, and serving as a minister in Alabama from 1934 to 1937. With the permission of the Presbytery, Meacham then joined the southern staff of the National Labor Relations Board, remaining with that agency for nine years. In 1946, he left the NLRB to become labor advisor to Lt. General John R. Hodge in Korea, an office he held ten months. Returning from Korea in 1947 he shortly thereafter joined the staff of the Amalgamated Clothing Workers of America as assistant to the president. It was from this union that Stewart Meacham found his way into the missionary work of the Methodist Church.

Mr. Meacham showed me a letter he had written Bishop G. Bromley Oxnam, explaining his idea of industrial missionaries to India. He had, he wrote, "a great desire to put the two halves of my life together—the church half and the labor movement half." He painted the picture of the need for such church-labor cooperation and forcefully pointed out how the church might help. His letter continued:

To an appalling degree we have let the impression develop in most of Asia that only the Communists are interested in social reform. The more I think about it, the more I believe that the Protestant Church could, if it would, play a role.

Would it be possible to develop a missionary activity in a country like India, say, which would embrace in its purpose the encouragement of improved industrial relations, better utilization of the land, increased interest in civil liberties, and related objectives? If so, I would like to have a part in such an effort.

Listening to Mr. Meacham as he outlined his ideas my thoughts returned to the modest beginning of this mountain school, which has now developed to the point where leaders of the Methodist Church chose it as a vehicle for teaching this young man the techniques of promoting community work in industrial centers.

Chapter VI

WORK AND COLOR

EVER SINCE I was a young woman beginning to think about the South with its injustices and inequalities, I have thought that it is not the Negro who has held the region back, but rather the shadow of the Negro which lies dark and distorted in the white man's mind.

That shadow has produced strange illusions which in their turn caused a breakdown in democracy and a tortured history for the South.

White people, in their fear, built protective barriers, so they thought, against the "encroachments of Negroes upon the special prerogatives of the whites." What they really built were road blocks to democracy and justice and equal opportunity. In so doing, they hurt all the South and all the people. The evil weeds that grow from oppression, poverty, and ignorance spread in many directions. Trying to "keep the Negro in his place," the white man darkened and impoverished the society in which he lived, and narrowed his own soul.

It is because of the CIO's concern for minorities, as well as for economically depressed people, that I was drawn to it from its beginning. This movement offers more to southern progress than any other. Through the fifteen years of CIO in the South, convention resolutions on equality and opportunity for all have become solid achievements.

The intangible—one might say spiritual—progress is equally real and even more important to a man's dignity and self respect. People become persons; human relationships are vastly improved. White men seeing their leaders greet a Negro visitor as "Mr. Jones," with extended right hand, follow the example and a new pattern is made.

The use of polite language and friendly greetings are far more significant than people living outside the South can know. The mere fact that groups of union folk, white and colored, are sitting down together all over the nation to discuss things of equal importance to all creates a new kind of fellowship—an interdependent bond—because they are seriously working together for the common good. Eating together at a hotel lunch or at a union barbecue is another spiritual experience for these union folk. There is balm for old sores in such simple, natural acts.

"In the CIO a common humanity has been substituted for discrimination. Witness the degree of healing brought about by the unions."

In the democracy of mixed meetings, Negroes vote for good white men and white men vote for competent Negroes. It is a heartening thing that both can share responsibilities as they seek to represent all and work for all. In these democratic processes the union is the corrective of 150 years of mistaken history.

A Mississippian said to me many years ago, "The CIO will never organize the South; Negroes just won't join unions; and the white people won't work in the same unions with Negroes." He was a false prophet. The CIO has stuck to the declaration written into its first convention resolutions in 1938: "To bring about the effective organization of the working men and women of America regardless of race, creed, color or nationality and to unite them for common action into labor unions for their mutual aid and protection."

It is an amazing and important fact that tens of thousands of southern white men and women are now enrolled in mixed unions. It was not easy to bring this about. The argument that brought most response in the beginning was that if employers hired colored workers the union must organize them, or they would be used to split one group from the other to the destruction of the union.

I was here in the South early enough to see the hesitant progress in these now integrated unions. Meetings were often held separately, with officers from each visiting the other, carrying reports of union actions and resolutions. Both groups voted.

Then there was one meeting for all, but the Negroes were waved to the rear of the hall, or to one side. There was variety in this pattern, but increasingly one mixed local got all of its members together to transact their business. In the beginning there might be "white" and "colored" water fountains. Now there is usually one. These divisive practices are now taboo in CIO unions, except in rare and frowned upon instances.

In a city where the divisions in seating and facilities are maintained, and the local union insists that city ordinances forbid mixed meetings, I know that top CIO leadership has done its utmost to end such divisions. One of the most powerful addresses I have heard Philip Murray make was hurled at one of these divided meetings—a rope separating one part of the hall from the other. Even as Mr. Murray pleaded for democracy and equality, that rope was cut here and there and soon trailed on the floor. White and colored men on the edges of the two groups filtered among one another, but no one was arrested.

Years ago when the going was particularly hard, I was in a CIO Council meeting in a Nashville hotel. As we broke up, the hotel manager informed Paul Christopher that any mixed meetings in the future would have to be held in a back room, reached by the freight elevator. Paul's reply was that we would meet elsewhere next time. Later on there developed many places where the two races could meet together.

In the beginning all union organizers were white. Now there are many Negro representatives both on the CIO staff and with national unions. The last CIO conference held by Mr. Bittner in Atlanta in 1949 was participated in by about twenty Negroes—staff men and delegates from local unions. Negroes were on the platform and one of them made an excellent address. A dinner meeting for all delegates had been arranged, but the hotel canceled the reservation at the last moment. No other dining place could be found so the dinner was called off. The time had passed when white union men banqueted while the Negro delegates fared as best they could.

The inner machinery of the union provides means of seeing that Negro members get justice without affront. The worker who feels he has not had a square deal can go to an officer in the union, who in turn can go to the top man of that union. Without any noise about it, the wrong is corrected. It has happened that the white union officer has been arrested and has gone to jail until bond was furnished. The colored workers look on with amazement, and are convinced that this white man's union is their union too and they can trust it to look after their interests.

There is more, beyond the union boundaries, won for southern Negroes. At the time of the first National Labor Relations Board hearing in Columbus, Georgia, when the textile workers were to vote for or against the Textile Workers Union, I recall an elderly Negro man who as he approached the ballot box stood still and looked up at the flag above it. He was so moved that he burst forth, "Look at that flag. It is the sign our government is behind us. I never was a citizen in these United States until now because I never could vote until my government gave me that right today."

At a union council meeting I sat next to the secretary of a new local composed of Negro women—no white person was employed in the small plant. I asked the secretary what was the most important thing she had gained through the union. "Respect," she replied in a flash. "The boss can't come out in the plant any more and yell at us, or fire us if we answer him. The union takes care of all that now."

Charlie Mathias has already told of the company which had long fought the union and more than 30 per cent of whose employees were Negroes. When they tried to split white from colored by offering an old-age pension for the colored considerably less than that for the whites, the union firmly refused the settlement. Indeed, the CIO has gone further than any organization I know in the South in promoting fair play and justice for minorities. Negro and white organizers get in a car to make a long trip. En route the white men will see that the colored representatives get food.

Sometimes the white people who want to know about the union ask for some one to come to talk with them. Near Macon such a group, mostly white, sat waiting for the organizer. Finally a Negro organizer appeared, expressed his regret that the white man sent for could not come, suggested that the white people leave and he would address the Negroes. None of this nonsense for the white would-be members—they insisted that the Negro stay and hold their meeting—which he did. A union grew out of this meeting.

Sometimes the plant management will refuse to meet with a bargaining or grievance committee if there are Negroes in it. The union represents all the workers and Negro participation is only fair. The white men stand by the colored until these situations are changed.

Out of all this have blossomed some of the most truly Christian attitudes it has been my joy to behold.

There have been intangible spiritual values worked out in the South as both races have managed to overcome the obstacles to practicing democracy and achieved a finer measure of brotherhood.

I have seen once deeply prejudiced white men throw off the fear and suspicion that made them question the CIO mandate of no discrimination. They have grown in stature as they met each situation on these principles.

I think Negro leadership is tolerant and understanding of the white man's efforts to make things square for the Negro workers. They realize that the white people are struggling to keep open the doors and ease off the strain of these new and friendly relations.

The stories of some of these Negro CIO leaders are told on the following pages.

WILLIAM DORSEY

When I first met Mr. Dorsey he was working with Fred Pieper, then CIO director of Louisiana. These two were organizing in and around New Orleans, and in Louisiana generally. I spoke to a number of their union meetings in those early organizing days.

Brother Dorsey is very dark, but luminous eyes shine out from under his massive brow. Because of his powerful frame, one does not realize how tall he is. He might well pose for a figure in some great labor building. Dorsey is a natural orator and has a strong religious conviction, linking economics and ethics with his spiritual faith. He combines an inspiring faith with native dignity and loftiness of soul.

Not long ago, Highlander Folk School made its facilities available to the National Religion and Labor Foundation for a week's school on the subject of religion and labor. Willie Dorsey, John Ramsay, and I were there and Brother Dorsey told us what the CIO meant to him. He said, "The CIO is the new emancipation to the workers of the South, especially to the southern Negro. The great crusade of the CIO in organizing Dixie is supporting a great cause for suffering humanity.

"I shall continue to work to build this union until I am ready to go to my just reward. Then I will be able to call my sons and tell them of the great struggles and hardships I have passed through. I have no silver and gold to leave them. I leave them only the CIO unions that will give them the benefits that my father and myself did not have in our youth—a better living, old age pensions and insurance paid by the boss, seniority rights—human dignity.

"I pray for God to guide the leaders of this great crusade which is the CIO organizing drive in Dixie."

There is a warm friendship between Willie Dorsey and John Ramsay, the Negro labor leader and the CIO's director of church and community relations. Each respects the spiritual power of the other, a power that carries them through overwhelmingly hard work and difficult situations. In response to a request from me, Brother Dorsey wrote me in July, 1951, to tell of one incident where Brother Ramsay had come to his rescue:

DEAR LADY:

Regarding your letter of July 7, I am always happy to tell the truth about what the CIO means to me, and the other millions of workers in the South.

I was working on the Stonewall Cotton Mills. The workers in this community had been driven into fear and poverty. Their wages were low, working conditions were horrible, their housing was bad, and they were unable to provide for themselves proper medical care.

In my efforts to organize these workers, I planned an organizational program, to which the workers of the Stonewall Cotton Mills and their children were invited. The bosses and the powers-that-be made no attempt to conceal the fact that they were opposed to such a program. Thus, fear and tension gripped the neighborhood.

Therefore, in order to offset this situation, I also invited the ministers and the leading people of the community. Knowing that Brother John Ramsay could contribute greatly in this type of situation, I naturally invited him.

On the day of the program, the workers and their children began to assemble and, to my surprise, there I was with nobody on the side of the union except me. I felt very much alone and somewhat defeated.

Suddenly, I looked up and saw Brother Ramsay coming down the road toward us. It was in the afternoon and the light was shining on him. . . . He reminded me of John the Baptist and of Jesus Christ, bringing a message of hope to a down-trodden people.

The mere presence of Brother Ramsay boosted my courage and made that one of the happiest moments of my life. As long as I live, I shall never forget the message that he delivered, calmly and reassuringly, to those workers, concerning the teaching of Jesus Christ as it relates to the objectives of the CIO.

His message to those workers was the turning point in our drive to organize Stonewall Cotton Mills. The workers voted overwhelmingly in favor of the CIO in the NLRB election.

OSCAR REESE THOMAS

Oscar Reese Thomas was the first Negro staff member of the United Steelworkers in the southern area. He won this appointment in April, 1944, by his effective service in organizing employees of industrial companies in Memphis, Tennessee, when he was a rank and file member of the union.

Mr. Thomas was born in Memphis, May 16, 1920. He evidently had an instinct for organizing people, for he aided in the organization of the Oliver Baptist Church in 1924, when he was only twenty-two years old. He is still a member of that church, where he has been secretary of the board of ushers and also served as deacon and trustee. He held the office of superintendent of the Sunday School for ten years, and was also church secretary for ten years, until his work as a union staff member took him away from Memphis and he had to give up the last two offices.

I asked him how he first became interested in the union. That was a long story, he said:

"I worked in the Orgill Brothers Hardware plant. My job was order clerk. I filled the orders as they came in. It was a wholesale house, handling hardware and furniture. I did my work and was frank in my dealings and always got along with the fellows I worked with. I worked there twenty-two years.

"One of the fellows from our plant got a job at Pidgeon Thomas and he came back and told us about the union and what it was getting for the people over there. Then some of the fellows in Orgill went to a union meeting of Pidgeon employees. They came back and told other people at Orgill's and that started organizing in our plant.

"The men had this organization well under way before they mentioned it to me, because I had been employed by the company so long they were skeptical about me. They invited me to come to a meeting and I accepted their invitation and went and listened to the information given by Steel Representatives Will Watts and Bill Henderson.

"After weighing this information carefully, I decided that the labor movement would not only help me, but help the other fellows working around me, who needed it more than I.

"For many evenings I had heard one of the foremen tell the men not to come back if they could not do more work than they had done that day. At that time they had started a speed-up system of piece work by giving contracts to the men to unload cars by the job. After checking this high rate of speed in unloading, the company wanted to hold the men to the speed-up system.

"At the expiration of the NRA all colored employees were carried to the basement. There they were told about the discontinuing of the NRA and the new rules of the company which said we would no longer work forty hours a week, but would have to make forty-six hours.

"Overtime rates after that were less than the regular hourly rate of pay. For instance, men who worked for thirty-seven cents as a regular daily hour's pay would get only twenty-five cents an hour for overtime. Sometimes they worked the men overtime with no pay for the extra time except fifty cents to buy supper.

"At the conclusion of the meeting in the basement we were told that if anyone did not like it he should speak then—for if there were any rotten apples in the barrel they wanted to get rid of them there.

"The company meeting in the basement answered a long question in my mind, because it showed the attitude of the superintendent toward the colored employees who had been with the company a long time. I saw why we needed a union and what it could do for us.

"There were many other things the company did that were not fair to the colored. The company had a practice that gave the colored a one-week vacation and the white two weeks. They also gave a bonus twice a year, the colored receiving one-half the amount the whites received. They gave picnics, parties, and dances to the white employees and none for the colored.

"All these practices were equalized when the United Steelworkers came into the plants. From that time on, I took an active part in the union.

"In Memphis as a whole, in most all locals the white and colored worked jointly in the same union. Sometimes these mixed unions had some colored officers, including the president. The first meeting I went to I was elected financial secretary. Later on they wanted to elect me as president. I objected, for this reason: to elect me president in place of the man who was holding that office, would make us lose him. In other words, he would quit the union. If he remained as president he would still have to abide by the decisions of the body, and I felt I was just as influential with the group as he was. So I remained as financial secretary until I left to join the staff of the Steelworkers.

"I want to speak about a spirit of religious devotion that is in these unions. Most of the local unions have ministers among their members, who work in the plant. One of these ministers will serve as chaplain to the local, and open and close the meetings with prayer. Religion is part of the life of the union.

"I came into the labor movement in the Steel Union under the leadership of Mr. Henderson and Mr. Watts. But our rapid progress came after Mr. Earl A. Crowder took over the Memphis area for the Steelworkers. Mr. Crowder got the steel locals to move their meeting place down town, and also to affiliate with the Memphis CIO Industrial Union Council.

"In April, 1944, I went on the staff of the Steelworkers' Union. I was then moved to Chattanooga and since then I have traveled all over District 35, of which Mr. W. H. Crawford is director.

"Since being on the staff, I have found that CIO has the most to offer the low-paid workers, especially in the South. This gives me double courage in trying to reach the colored brothers wherever I am assigned to work, for I know that the workers have all to gain and nothing to lose in voting themselves into the CIO.

"For the union is the only salvatioin of the working man, and the CIO is the only organization in the South that advocates, and has, joint meetings of both races in any section they enter."

John Henry Hall

John Henry Hall had to assume responsibility for himself and his family early in life. He made a brave effort to complete his high school education, but had to give it up to go to work. Not discouraged by seeing the difficulties in bringing up a family, he married young and has five children and three grandchildren.

John Henry has seen what unions can do to build family life on a sound economic basis and has thrown himself, heart and soul, into helping organize the unorganized.

He has been on the staff of the Packinghouse Workers for some years, and feels that the union has done a great deal to bring about better understanding and good relations between the white and Negro races. Here he tells his own story.

"I was born in Glascock County, Georgia. At the age of fifteen I moved with my family to Daytona Beach, Florida. I lived in New Smyrna and Lake City, Florida, later. In 1929 I moved to Birmingham, Alabama, and it was there that I joined my first local union. I lived in Birmingham until I was assigned to the UPWA staff and was transferred to Atlanta, Georgia.

"I was working for the Alabama Packing Company, then located in Birmingham, at the time the CIO started its organizational campaign in the South in 1937. I was a butcher and was drawing what at that time represented the highest wages paid to any employee in the plant. However, even the highest wage in the Alabama Packing Company was hardly a sufficient amount to support me and my family.

"My first personal contact with the CIO was one day when one of the Steelworkers' representatives drove a truck with a loud-speaker in front of our place and made a talk to the people at the plant. He appeared at the plant for about three consecutive days at the noon hour and talked to the workers while we were eating lunch. Soon after that a meeting was called and we formed a union.

"The company engaged in their usual tactics and, although we had formed ourselves into a pretty strong group, they would not bargain with us in good faith and we were unable to negotiate a satisfactory agreement. In fact we had no contract. All that we had was a memorandum of agreement signed by the company stating what they would do. But frankly they would not even live up to that.

"The union I belonged to was an Amalgamated local with membership in the Armour Plant (the old Birmingham Packing Company), the Star Provision Packing Company, and the Alabama Packing Company. We did not have a real union until, in 1940, Mr. G. R. Hathaway, who at that time was the only representative of the Packinghouse Workers Organizing Committee in the South, was assigned to work with us in Birmingham. It was at this time that we began to build ourselves into a real strong union and began to take positive action. We of the Alabama Packing Company and the Star Provision Packing Company acquired our first signed contract in September, 1940.

"While we had been negotiating for a considerable period of time, the company was antagonistic and arbitrary in their position and was unwilling to agree to any of our demands that represented real contract gains. As a last resort we felt we had to strike.

"I remember vividly the negotiations on the evening of the day that we went on strike. Mr. Max Goldberg, who was the company owner and manager of the plant, sat with a big cigar in his mouth telling the committee and Mr. Hathaway what he would and would not do. I remember Mr. Hathaway's telling Mr. Goldberg that the local union was going to have a meeting that night and that he was going to recommend that the workers go on strike if Mr. Goldberg did not agree to the terms of the contract we were discussing. Mr. Goldberg only laughed and said he wasn't worried and that he felt confident the employees of the Alabama Packing Company would not go on strike. Was he surprised! For that night the membership, having met prior to the hour of midnight, agreed that as of midnight they would go on strike. At the agreed upon hour, the membership of both shifts in the Alabama Packing Company and the Star Provision Company assembled in front of the respective plants.

"In less than one hour after the strike was called, Mr. Goldberg appeared on the scene quite excited, demanding to see Mr. Hathaway, who as a matter of fact had gone to his hotel to sleep. We got in touch with Mr. Hathaway and at something around two o'clock in the morning an agreement was reached and the night shift returned to work.

"After reaching an agreement with the Alabama Packing Company Plant, Mr. Hathaway, members from the Star Provision Packing Company, and I went over to that plant where we contacted Mr. Gottleib, owner and operator, and there we reached an agreement with this group also.

"Although we had gotten our first signed contract with both companies, our troubles as such were not over by any means. We were hounded by the police department and other law-enforcement groups. For some time we tried holding our meetings in the Jefferson County Courthouse located in the city of Birmingham. But we could not hold satisfactory meetings there because they could not be private. It was nothing unusual for the deputies to come into our meetings and order the Negro officers, of whom I was one, from behind the desk. These deputies would say that in the state of Alabama and in the county of Jefferson they were never going to allow 'Niggers' to sit behind desks and officiate at meetings. For a period of several years we were harassed in this manner. However, eventually we were able to get our own union hall where we conducted meetings without segregation with a minimum of interference from the law-enforcement group in the city of Birmingham.

"You can well understand that these were signal victories for us: (1) contracts as such; and (2) our ability to hold meetings without segregation and operate under the policy of CIO. It is a fact that during these years CIO union meetings were the only places where segregation was not practiced. I know that in all AF of L meetings segregation existed and so far as I know, it is practiced in most AF of L unions in Birmingham even until this day.

"I served as an officer of the first local union set up by the Packinghouse Workers Organizing Committee in the capacity of recording secretary. I served my local union as an officer until such a time as I was assigned as a full-time staff member. Prior to that assignment I served as a part-time organizer, and I am glad to say that by the end of 1943 we had all of the major packing companies in Birmingham organized. In addition to my duties as recording secretary I served as a member of the negotiating committee and on the grievance committee of the Alabama Packing Company plant. I was also elected and served as a member of the executive board of the Birmingham Industrial Union Council, in the capacity of trustee.

"Eventually I was assigned by Mr. Hathaway to Atlanta and I worked with him in organizing the Atlanta plants and many of the plants in South Georgia. It has been my pleasure to see the growth of the United Packinghouse Workers of America, CIO, from less than three hundred people with contracts in three plants in Birmingham to a dues-paying membership in this District 9 of over five thousand members, some thirty-five local unions and approximately seventy-five contracts. I feel that our efforts have not been in vain and, although the UPWA is a relatively young organization, I firmly believe that we are on our way to being one of the major unions of CIO.

"Certainly it gives me the greatest of pleasure to know that I, a Negro, can work and serve the interests of our membership even in the South. And when I look at people these days who are well-fed, well-paid, and well-clothed, as well as being well-housed, and I know that these things have come about because of their being able to belong to the CIO union and particularly the UPWA, my heart swells with pride. I am even more glad that though I am a Negro it has been possible, through my own efforts and those of others of my own race, to bring about a greater understanding and closer relationship between the white and Negro races, particularly in the South."

Chapter VII

THE CHURCHES

IN THE first quarter of this century there was war between the coal and steel barons and their employees. When men tried to relieve their terrific working and living conditions by organizing unions, the heads of the great industries used all means to stamp them out regardless of the lives it cost.

The conscience of the nation was aroused by the investigation and report of the Interchurch World Movement on the Steel Strike of 1919. The revelations of this report influenced the churches and contributed to the industrial pronouncements of their Social Creeds. These creeds usually included a statement on the right of employees to form labor unions for purposes of collective bargaining. Today there are but few exceptions to this.

In the early period of the southern drive that began in 1937, CIO unions were frequently attacked by mill village preachers or free-lance evangelists. The large new tents that appeared in communities where the Textile Workers Union was organizing indicated financing beyond the ability of the preacher conducting the revival.

Sincerely religious men in the unions proved useful allies in combating religious fanatics. Our organizers asked me for church statements in behalf of the right to bargain and I prepared my first leaflet of the sort in 1942, calling it "The Churches and Labor Unions." In 1945 I edited a leaflet with the same title, of which 40,000 copies were used by many CIO unions. More recently, John

Ramsay and I spent considerable time on two publications of this sort.

A minister's daughter and granddaughter, and a member of the Episcopal Church, I early developed a concern for the application of religion to social injustices. So I have taken a special delight in bringing the pronouncements of the Social Creeds to church people.

As a delegate at large from the Protestant Episcopal Church, I attended the National Study Conference on the Church and Economic life held in Pittsburgh in 1947. This conference "suggested that official church bodies, both denominational and inter-denominational, face the moral issues of the economic order of our day and make pronouncements about them which can be transmitted to local church groups for study and action."

This conference was significant because "never before had official church bodies joined in a national undertaking devoted entirely to the relation of the churches and Christian people to economic life." The great labor unions and the National Association of Manufacturers were there. Ministers were present. The delegates were predominantly lay men and women, representing broad groups.

Much of the conference dealt with the question of whether religion and the churches should or should not have a concern for economic matters. I took an active part in these discussions, which carried the churches further in commitments on participation in economic matters than ever before.

A MINISTER CHANGES HIS MIND

When I went with the CIO in 1937, one of my first acts was to send out 500 letters to southern ministers, enclosing the Labor Day Message of the Federal Council of Churches. The message said, in part,

It is because of the concern of religion for justice and for social welfare that Church bodies have for thirty years officially declared for the right of employees as well as employers to organize. . . . Experience has shown that since industry is often organized on a national or even wider basis, labor unions of corresponding scope are needed if workers are to be adequately represented in truly democratic relations, and if industry-wide standards are to be maintained.

This led to considerable correspondence and useful new contacts. A few ministers were indignant at my linking the church and the labor unions. On the other hand, it brought a few invitations to speak to church groups, and several ministers asked me to send them information about the unions to enable them to mention the message in their sermons on Labor-Day Sunday. The most significant response came from the chairman of the Social Service Commission of the Southern Baptist Church, Dr. Arthur James Barton, who was pastor of a leading church in Wilmington, N. C. Dr. Barton was long considered a leader in the Baptist Convention and as chairman of the Social Service Commission he was in a position to influence the entire body.

He asked in his first letter if the Federal Council of Churches had sent me its Labor Day message for distribution. I replied no, I had bought 500 copies and distributed them myself, following a practice I had begun in Richmond. He expressed strong disapproval of the CIO and thought it was perhaps the duty of ministers to express their opinion in favor of the AF of L and against the CIO.

I replied asking if he would refrain from any public comment until I had had an opportunity to talk with him. He consented to this and gave me an appointment between revival services he was holding near Wilmington. So that city became one of my chief objectives in my first long automobile trip.

This was probably the most important contact with a minister that it was possible for me to make, and as I approached Wilmington that September afternoon in a humble frame of mind, I prayed for guidance in the coming interview. If I could not convince Dr. Barton of the values in the CIO, he might become a powerful opponent.

Next morning I was at Dr. Barton's home at ten o'clock. While awaiting him my eyes fell on a fine picture of General Robert E. Lee. The tall, white-haired, elderly minister gave me a friendly greeting and before I plunged into the conversation, I told him how much I liked the General's picture, which I said was much better than the one that had hung on my family's sitting-room wall.

Dr. Barton was interested in this statement and expressed the highest admiration of General Lee. I told him that Lee and father's mother, Lucy Randolph, were first cousins, and there were various other ties of kinship between him and both my mother and father. After that he beamed upon me and I was securely wrapped in the Confederate flag.

The good man was pleased when I told him that as a boy, father adored his famous cousin and used to listen in rapt attention as the General talked with the ladies of the household after their evening meal. Father said that Lee always withdrew to the parlor with the ladies when the other men remained in the dining room talking over their wine. The General said he preferred the company of the "fair sex." Of course, I told Dr. Barton that father and all of his brothers were in the Confederate Army.

There was a spark of congeniality that made the talk with Dr. Barton a pleasant one. He listened with interest to what I said about the CIO and frankly told me that his opinion of it was based on local newspapers and occasional magazine articles. He had never before met a representative of industrial unions. He promised to read literature if I would send it to him, and to keep an open mind about the CIO.

We talked about the ministers I knew in the Baptist churches and the Episcopalians he knew. He was incredulous when I told him that considerable research on my part had not revealed Southern Baptist Convention action endorsing the right of labor to organize and bargain collectively. He was sure I was wrong, for he remembered the year that such a resolution had been adopted and had had a part in it. He promised to verify this, and if indeed no such action had been taken he would get the Social Service Commission to take up the matter at the next Convention.

Just before the 1938 Convention, Dr. Barton wrote me, "I think you are going to like the Convention resolution on collective bargaining that will be adopted at Richmond." Soon after that I received from him a copy of the aforesaid resolution. The Baptists said:

We recognize the right of labor to organize and to engage in collective bargaining to the end that labor may have a fair and living wage, such as will provide *not only* for the *necessities* of life, but for *recreation, pleasure,* and *culture.* (Italics mine.)

The Southern Baptist Church had moved most slowly in adopting a resolution on labor's right to organize, but when they moved, though acting last, they gave the best of all.

From that time on until his death a few years later, Dr. Barton used to call me when he was in Atlanta, and we had lunch together. I have missed this pleasant friendship.

MINISTER-ORGANIZER

In looking for the beginning of CIO unions in the South, I went to see my friend Reverend Charles W. Webber, of Richmond, Virginia. Charlie is not old in years or ideas, but he is rich in his understanding of the needs of working people and why they should organize. He is still a Methodist minister and occasionally holds services. He is on the staff of the Amalgamated Clothing Workers of America, and president of the Virginia Industrial Union Council.

While teaching at the Union Theological Seminary in New York, Dr. Webber first became interested in the labor movement and in consequence spent much time in volunteer organizing. He was so successful in this work that when there was a hard nut to crack in Richmond, the Amalgamated requested him to spend a summer vacation organizing the employees of Friedman-Harry Marks in Richmond.

It took more than one vacation to carry this organizing campaign to a successful conclusion, but it was done and well done. Dr. Webber worked among the people in an educational way—they came to know just what unions meant, why they must be, and how they lift the level of living among working people.

This good minister also turned to his own profession for help in bringing unionism to the clothing workers of Richmond. The result was that the Methodist Ministers' Association upheld the collective bargaining section of the Methodist Book of Discipline, and stood by the pronouncements of this church as applied to the garment workers' efforts to organize.

Some of the ministers attended union meetings and spoke to them or asked a blessing. When the company fired many people for joining the union, a relief committee was set up to distribute funds given by the Amalgamated. Reverend Henry Lee Robinson was active in this relief work and won many friends. Without a strike or work stoppage, the employees of Friedman-Harry Marks won a good collective bargaining agreement. Today that agreement stands, with modern improvements added, as the guarantee of good working relations between the approximately one thousand workers and the company.

Dr. Webber is justly proud of the splendid labor-management relations that continue to exist. Indeed, Richmond is proud of this outstanding achievement, which is in accord with the Amalgamated's determination to have no strikes once a union agreement is reached, but to settle all differences through conciliation and arbitration.

PREACHER JONES'S RELIGION

Early in 1946, I was asked to go to a small mill village in South Carolina, where several violations of civil rights had occurred. I was also asked to look into the facts concerning a preacher who was being used by the textile companies to intimidate union people. The problems of civil rights were easily dealt with, but the preacher was the really tough man in town. His home and church were on the edge of the village, but his financial interest and religion were dominated by the mill management. Let's call him Preacher Jones.

The preacher had obtained from mill management a list of all the employees who had joined the union—and it was a large number. One morning after a Sunday service, the preacher said he had a special message for union members and requested them to stay after the service. He first made a vicious attack on the CIO, calling it all the bad names he could think of, and finished with a declaration that no CIO members could be "saved" and that the people would have to decide between the church and the union. Union members were not welcome and would not be accepted in the church, he declared. As a result there was a large withdrawal from the union.

I went to call on Jones accompanied by Fred Wingard, the CIO representative who was taking me around in his car. Fred was born and raised in that vicinity, and had, upon his return from the war, gone to work with the Textile Workers Union.

After several calls, we finally found preacher Jones at his home. He is a large, muscular, black-haired, black-eyed individual with a forbidding expression. He appeared to be anything but the sort of man one would want as a spiritual adviser, or a friend in time of need.

Sitting in a large, stuffed armchair, the "reverend" glared at Fred and me with intense hostility, and expressed his belief that the CIO and all its unions and members were offspring of the devil. It proved almost impossible to talk to him, for he interrupted everything Fred or I said by asking some irrelevant question.

Finally, the preacher dropped his bull-like head and hunching forward said to me, "You don't believe in no right kind of religion— you believe in a social religion and that ain't Christianity. I don't believe in no social religion."

I, too, leaned forward and asked earnestly, but politely, "Then you don't believe in the teachings of Jesus? How can you be a Christian . . ." Interrupting me, he shouted, "Yes, I do believe the teachings of Jesus; that's just what I do believe."

"But," I insisted, "you can't believe in what Jesus taught if you do not have a social religion. His whole life, His teachings, and His death were all part of a great social religion. Jesus said the commandment to love your neighbor as yourself was second only to the commandment to love God with all one's heart and mind and soul."

Preacher Jones was lost for an answer. I reminded the preacher that at the Last Judgment, Jesus said men would be judged by what they had done to their fellow men and I expanded this theme. The direct quotations from the Bible took the steam out of Mr. Jones's discourse, but about this time I saw a woman standing in the dining room and peeping through the crack in the door. Seeing her husband in a state of confusion, his red-haired, sharp-tongued wife came into the room and ordered Fred and me to leave so her husband could eat his dinner.

When this virago came in, Fred and I arose and walked in a leisurely way toward the front door. At the door we stopped and I tried to tell the pair of them that some day when workers were organized in unions, as they would surely be, they would remember who had been their friends and who their enemies.

As the wife's face grew angrier and her tongue sharper, Fred and I remained quietly polite. Mrs. Jones had reached the state of flinging all the abuse she could think of, but we left smiling. I have often thought of that pair and what would have happened if the woman had started scratching my face, as seemed possible just before we left.

GOD'S GOOD MAN

For some years I had been hearing about and wanting to know John G. Ramsay, then director of church and community relations for the United Steelworkers of America. But he worked in other sections and lived in Columbus, Ohio.

Finally, John and I met at the National Study Conference on The Churches and a Just and Durable Peace, at Cleveland, Ohio, in January, 1945. After the first session in which I had spoken from the floor, I saw a tall, good-looking man with a light upon his face descending upon me with outstretched hand, and saying,

"At last I am meeting Lucy Mason."

I responded, "And at last I am meeting John Ramsay." Our friendship began then and has deepened in the intervening years.

This was a conference called by The Federal Council of Churches of Christ in America. Mr. Ramsay had been elected a delegate both by the Presbyterian Church, U. S. A. laymen, and the Laymen's Movement for a Christian World. I had been appointed by the Right Reverend St. George Tucker, Presiding Bishop of the National Council of the Protestant Episcopal Church.

In the following years, John and I were both sent as delegates from our churches to three more national conferences on The Churches and Economic Life and one on The Churches and World Order. We also were visiting delegates to the Constituting Convention of the National Council of the Churches of Christ in the U. S. A., which took place in Cleveland, November 28-29 and December 1, 1950.

In the several hundred delegates to that first conference, there were, I think, only three or four from labor. Later conferences have had many labor men. The list of church committees to which Mr. Ramsay now belongs shows that this great Christian layman has won an important place in church councils.

John Ramsay's name has appeared in church papers, more perhaps than that of any other labor layman. The *Christian Herald* of September, 1949, carried a beautiful story of John by Kenneth L. Wilson, entitled, "Portrait of a Labor Leader." With characteristic modesty, Mr. Ramsay finds it difficult to talk freely enough about himself. So, for a picture of Mr. Ramsay's religious life I am quoting freely from the *Christian Herald*.

John G. Ramsay was born on a Friday the thirteenth. No one has suffered any particular ill fortune as a result—except, maybe, those armorplated skeptics who persist in discounting the proposition that zeal for Christianity and zeal for labor can dwell peaceably and without embarrassment under the same hatband.

It may come as a surprise to the skeptics on both sides to learn that their distrust of each other has been mutual. If some churches have mistakenly regarded all labor unions as a front for Communism and social upheaval, some labor groups also have mistakenly regarded all churches as a front for management and the status quo.

Forty-seven-year-old John Ramsay has done more perhaps than any other one man to bring churches and labor close enough together to weep repentantly on one another's shoulders. . . .

And, for the workers, he has been digging out the social pronouncements of denominational conventions and general assemblies, and has proved to labor bodies large and small that the church is not nearly as stuffily unaware of social justice as they may have thought. The result has been a lot of unclenched fists and handshaking all around. Of course, Ramsay, as a labor missionary to the church and vice versa, still has to cover a good deal of virgin territory, but he has a long stride! . . .

In short, John Ramsay looks like any other man who senses that there is a task to be done in this world and that he, as a follower of the Christ, is morally obliged to have a part in it. . . .

If by any chance some might think they were dealing with a radical with Red ideas, he would soon disabuse them of that fear. . . .

He would say, as he said to this reporter: "Early in my experience in the labor movement, I realized that some of the Communists in America were infiltrating into union leadership through active participation in the democracy of the labor movement. Recently, in a local situation in which I was helping to break the Communist control of a local union I received this question during a radio broadcast: 'Would you say there is any particular method for maintaining the democratic American ideals?' To that I replied, 'If any minority group, such as Communists or Fascists, become powerful enough in America to be considered a threat to our democracy, it is because we as Christians in America who are a majority have shirked our duty.' ". . .

Mr. Ramsay's decision to dedicate his life to raising economic standards everywhere did not mean the tough going was over; many times there would be doubts that could be resolved only by application of the sternest faith. "I have no cut-and-dried program," John Ramsay puts it. "I ask God for guidance in everything I do. This, I find, releases a power that helps amazingly in even the smallest matters." . . .

Mr. Ramsay often speaks of the tendency of union members to doff their insignia when they go to church. No one there knows they are union men. But it works the other way, too. "The people who are not articulate about the union in the church are not articulate about their church in their union," he has found. . . .

Organized labor, as Ramsay convincingly explains it, is trying to make men feel like men. They are not out for paternalism. All that paternalism does is to make one man feel like a man. To live, a man must be able to give. It is every man's right to earn enough so that he can give—in all the little ways that are so important to the dignity of the human spirit.

John Ramsay is indisputedly on solid ground when he says, "I feel the church has a job to do to educate both labor and management as to its social vision."

His family has solid ground under it, too. One day Mrs. Ramsay overheard Dicky in a discussion with a neighbor's boy. "Who's the boss in your house—your mother or father?" the neighbor boy asked.

Dicky said, without having to think twice, "God is boss in our house."

The *Christian Herald* has given a beautiful story of John Ramsay's spiritual life. I now turn to John himself for the rest of his story.

"I was born in Howe, Oklahoma, leaving there before any recollection when the family moved to East Tennessee. As a boy I attended the Sunday School in the Fourth Presbyterian Church, U. S. A., in Knoxville.

"During World War I the family moved to Bethlehem, Pennsylvania. There as a young man, I became a leader in the Young People's Society of Christian Endeavor. There I learned to speak, to plan and conduct meetings, and to bridge denominational gaps between myself and the rest of the youth I met at school.

"It was in Bethlehem that I met and later married Gertrude E. Martin, a student at the Moravian College for Women. She was born in Nicaragua where her parents had been missionaries of the Moravian Church. As parents, we learned during the depression years that poverty in the midst of God's abundance is sinful and can ruin the strength of coming generations.

"As a steelworker for seventeen years, I learned to know the need for the union and to recognize that its work for the well-being of my fellowmen is a vital part in building the democratic way of life and the Kingdom of God. In June, 1936, with the setting up of the Steelworkers Organizing Committee of the CIO, I joined the union, becoming the first president of a Bethlehem Steel Local, CIO.

"President Philip Murray, Vice-President Van A. Bittner, and Secretary-Treasurer David J. McDonald, John V. Riffe, and other leaders of the United Steelworkers of America knew of my religious convictions and experiences. They gave me the opportunity I have had to work for the union and the church.

"During our early years I was asked to leave our local Presbyterian congregation because I accepted the presidency of the CIO union. Mrs. Ramsay, in another experience, was rudely ignored at a Presbyterian Women's meeting because of the union drive in that town. In the first case, we were convinced that the church belonged to Jesus, our Christ, and that we would be letting His church down by leaving. With reference to the other incident, Mrs. Ramsay received a strange apology from the women's leader who said, 'We should have realized you are not responsible for what your husband does!' From both of these experiences we learned to understand some of the love and patience of Jesus.

"Miss Mason has told of our meeting in Cleveland, Ohio at the National Conference on The Churches and a Just and Durable Peace in 1945. Before coming to the South I had already heard of Lucy Randolph Mason and her work as public relations representative of the CIO in the South. Both of us had learned, before we heard of each other, that the various religious bodies, more than thirty years before the unions gained legal status in the United States, had, with prophetic vision, endorsed that right in their social pronouncements. Lucy Mason and I have in recent years edited together two pamphlets—"Religion Speaks to Labor" and "The Churches and Brotherhood"—in which we are happy to be able to show that nearly all religious denominations in America are united in their expressed social convictions regarding unions and race.

"Shortly after the 1945 Conference, I came to Atlanta to address a Religion and Labor Fellowship luncheon group that had been arranged by Lucy Mason, with the help of Bill Crawford, southeastern director of the United Steelworkers of America, and Dr. H. B. Trimble, dean of the Candler School of Theology, Emory University. Here the leaders of Religion and the leaders of Labor began to know each other as persons and to understand the aims and aspirations of each others' organizations. Five years later this R.L.F. group in Atlanta is still meeting at a monthly luncheon, as do other similar groups in many towns and cities across the United States. With the permission of the group, Ray Warwick, Southern Editor of *Steel Labor*, has taken pictures and written the story of Religion and Labor Fellowships for one million steelworkers. These pictures tell a story of brotherhood, religion of all faiths, labor of all unions, and both groups interracial, meeting, eating, and enjoying fellowship with each other.

"Shortly after the original R.L.F. luncheon in Atlanta, I was invited by Van A. Bittner to join the CIO Organizing Committee and move my family to Georgia.

"We found a home at Lithia Springs near Atlanta where we joined the nearby Lithia Springs Methodist Church. Our oldest child, Patricia, was a sociology major at Ohio State University where she graduated cum laude. She now is Mrs. Earl A. Todt and lives in Columbus, Ohio. Labor Day morning 1949 she presented her labor father with his first grandson and this year we also have a granddaughter. John, Bill, and Dick grew to love Georgia and Douglasville High School. All of them are now students of Berea College, Berea, Kentucky.

"Since coming to the South, I have spent much time in bringing about a better understanding of labor by the communities in which our unions are at work. On the national scene I have accepted responsibility in the work of the church as follows:
layman—Lithia Springs, Georgia, Methodist Church; member— Commission on Evangelism, Presbyterian Church, U. S. A.; director —Laymen's Movement for a Christian World; co-chairman—National Religion and Labor Foundation; member—Fellowship of Southern Churchmen; visitor—Convention Catholic Committee of the South; serving on divisions, departments, and committees of the National Council of Churches of Christ in the United States of America: (1) Business and Finance Committee; (2) Department of Church and Economic Life; (3) Division of Christian Life and Work; (4) General Department of United Church Men, Executive Committee.

"Articles by me have appeared in many church papers: The *Christian Herald, Zion's Herald, Adult Student, Presbyterian Life,* The Evangelical and Reformed *Messenger, The Witness,* The Disciples of Christ *Evangelist, Christian Laymen, Guidepost, The Upper Room, Armed Forces Prayer Book, Laymen Speaking,* and so forth.

"In recent years I have given a week to the National Preaching Mission of the National Council of Churches and have in the past two years been a part of the Mission Team in Toledo, Ohio, and Tulsa, Oklahoma. I have done the same in the College Religious Emphasis Week, serving on the Team at Montevallo, Alabama, State College, and the University of Mississippi."

RELIGION AND LABOR FELLOWSHIP

John Ramsay has spoken of the Atlanta Religion and Labor Fellowship luncheon which he addressed soon after we met in Cleveland in 1945. W. H. Crawford and I had set up this luncheon, the first for the local group, which is still meeting monthly.

The first chairman in Atlanta was Dean H. B. Trimble of the Candler School of Theology. The present chairman is Major Vincent Cunningham, and the secretary is Ethel Stanley, who is on the staff of the Community Relations Department, CIO.

The Atlanta Religion and Labor Fellowship, as is the case with other similar luncheon groups in the South, is an interfaith, inter-union, and interracial experience. It is building bridges between religion and labor on which each can cross to the other.

These groups are now affiliating with the National Religion and Labor Foundation, whose aims and purposes are given in Article 2 of its Constitution:

To define the social teachings of our religious faith and apply them to our economic and industrial life.

To deepen the sense of religious commitment and vocation among all who work. To promote the general welfare through economic justice and maintenance and extension of civil liberties for people every-where, without regard to race, creed, color, or national origin.

To help the religious and labor movements interpret their aims and programs to one another and to bring them into relations of mutual understanding and cooperation.

To help the forces of religion and labor to discover and apply the techniques of social action that will achieve the ideals of our demo-cratic faith.

To encourage and support the organization of the unorganized, and to defend the trade union movement when attacked by forces that would destroy it.

To resist totalitarianism whether expressed in fascistic, communistic, or monopoly capitalistic forms.

The officers of the Foundation are: honorary president, Dr. John Haynes Holmes, New York; co-chairman for Religion, Reverend Francis W. McPeek, Chicago; co-chairman for Labor, John G. Ramsay, Atlanta; treasurer, Waldo E. Rasnake, Atlanta; executive director, Reverend Joseph W. Merchant, Columbus, Ohio; associate director, Dr. Witherspoon Dodge, Atlanta.

THE HELLO GIRL

It seems appropriate to conclude this chapter with the thinking of a young member of the Communications Workers Union. It was my good luck when at Highlander Folk School in the spring of 1951 to share a room with a member of this young telephone union, Miss Louise Cudd of Lynchburg, Va.—a charming and intelligent girl and ardent union member.

Louise had come to the religion and labor fellowship week at Highlander as a delegate from her local union—open-eyed and open-minded to learn all she could.

When the conference had been going two or three days, and there was a warm discussion of the relation between labor and religion, someone asked Louise why she had come. She replied:

"This invitation intrigued me because I had never before heard of a religion and labor organization. I had heard there was a connection between labor and religion and I was anxious to find out what it was.

"My educational director for division 33, Jules Pagano, had told me that some people in the labor movement feel it is their calling to help bring about the millennium, and that the labor movement had its basis on a quotation from Isaiah. That interested me also and I wanted to know about it."

A few months later Louise wrote me more about her thoughts on religion and labor.

"I resigned my post as educational director of our local. . . . I find legislative work as interesting and necessary as educational work, and the two are interrelated. It is the same with religion and labor. I don't think one can separate them, for to live for one is to work for the other. One of the greatest needs, I feel, is for us as union members to realize our responsibilities as Christian citizens."

Chapter VIII

THE MEANING

RECENTLY I received a letter from Franz Daniel, CIO director for North Carolina and one of our most experienced and able men, in which he evaluated my work with the CIO, particularly in the hard early days. Though too complimentary to me, this letter expresses so well what the CIO was intended to be, that, with some diffidence, I am including it here, feeling it is a valid part of the history of the CIO in the South.

Dear Miss Lucy:

Back in the Summer of 1937 Steve Nance called me down the hall to his office to tell me that you were coming to work with us. He told me who you were and what you were going to do for the then infant CIO. Steve was a careful man; when he lined out a person's character and capabilities—you knew that person pretty well. And Steve spent a long time talking about you. He talked about American history, and the part Virginia played; he fitted the names you bear into that recital of history. He was proud that you were going to be associated with us.

But the thing that Steve Nance knew best of all was the scope and importance of the fight we were then just beginning—the struggle to bring decency into the lives and homes of mill and factory workers. And I remember very well the certainty with which Steve dealt with the contribution you were going to make in that struggle. It ought to be a source of great pride to you, Miss Lucy, to know and to recognize the validity of the work you accomplished in that time. Steve Nance broke his heart in that campaign. But it would have been broken much earlier had it not been for the strength of your character and of your work.

I'm certain that you think back very often about your experiences in those early days. But I'm not at all sure that you recognize in yourself the changes that the years have wrought in you. The great thing about you, Miss Lucy, is that you have become experienced without having become cynical. Do you remember in our early conversations your conviction as to the "goodness" and "liberalism" of several southern industrialists we talked about by name? Before long you were helping to organize the mills owned by some of those same gentlemen. And I have watched your face as you looked at beaten union pickets. You have known at first hand the power that mill owners have at their disposal—and you have seen that power used in relentless force. And I don't think that any suspicion of hate has ever entered your thinking.

You have witnessed many times the disintegration of personal character. You have seen men fail to measure up—some through cowardice, some through corruption, but most through just plain weariness. And I have never known you to be shaken in your determination; or in your calm knowledge that somehow some day men would live self-respecting lives in more pleasant surroundings. That contribution of serene yet tough certainty as to our ultimate success is, to me, your greatest accomplishment. And you have accomplished that by being a part of the fight but at the same time refusing to allow yourself to be besmirched by those things that all too often leave marks on the participants in this fight.

These past fifteen years have been hard years for CIO organizers in the South. We're a long way from accomplishing those goals we talked about back in 1937. But we have made some gains. As a matter of fact we have every right to be proud of what we have accomplished. And no one has done more than you to make that statement possible. And take it from a case-hardened, battle-scarred old veteran like myself —we appreciate what you have done. I don't want to drift off into sentimentality, but I do want to add just one note of personal appreciation: the spiritual side of the labor movement is every bit as important as the economic. And it's the part that is so easy to lose sight of. There are many, many times that your presence and your faith have kept my vision clear and my understanding more certain.

We are going to continue the job we set out to do. In the failures, setbacks, gains, and victories ahead of us you will be present, as always. There is no question as to the emergence in time of a powerful labor movement in the South. . . .   Fraternally yours,

FRANZ E. DANIEL

There is a frequent argument as to whether the intangible social values brought by union membership are most important, or if unionism is still a matter of economic reward through wages and other financial benefits, such as pensions. Even now when wages are higher than ever before (but bitten into deeply by rising prices), this argument still goes on. Certainly wages are important, for they determine whether or not a man can adequately support his family, provide it with a better way of life and have something left for savings, education, and recreation.

In times of depression and unemployment unions are essential, and without them to set a base to wages, we would have an economic swamp as competing industries lowered wages to give them a more advantageous position. The great depression years ago is witness to this.

There is a third incentive for joining a union—men's social instinct, their urge to be part of something, to join a fellowship that seems worth while. This instinct and the persuasiveness of the fellow who talked the union cause get many a worker to join. In a way, the union takes the place that the Rotary Club and others play in a higher economic group.

In June, 1937, I wrote a good friend, Dr. Frank P. Graham, then president of the University of North Carolina, now on a United Nations mission to India. I told him I was coming with the CIO, and asked his advice on my plan of work. He commended my choice and expressed his faith in the organized labor movement as a contribution to society.

Dr. Graham taught history for many years. He must have studied some economics too, judging by his practical knowledge—in his case one could call it social-economics. His letter to me was an encouraging reminder of historic truths. He said in part—

Democracy is now at work in its third great historic period, first in the church, then in the state, and now in industry. Ecclesiastical autocracy yielded to collective agreements. Political absolutism was subjected to the collective bargaining incorporated in the Bill of Rights.

Economic autocracy must also give way to collective agreements between those who own and manage and those who do the work.

The autocratic system in industry remains in effect until employees get together in duly constituted unions which have, and exercise, the right to engage in collective bargaining through their elected committees and officers.

The exercise of joint industry-union machinery substitutes cooperative and beneficial action for the former autocratic authority of management. The social-economic pyramid has undergone some shifting. The small group of owners and managers at the apex find people from the base of the pyramid rising nearer the top and becoming articulate. Authority is now being shared through forces inside the union and political processes in the community.

To the public, "collective bargaining" is an obscure phrase, whereas to the union it means a democratic way of determining the terms of a union-management agreement. Unions carry on their business through elected committees, their chosen representatives meeting with management's representatives to work things out. After an agreement is arrived at, it must be submitted to the membership for approval.

One shift of power in the union's favor is knowledge of the facts when negotiating with management. Time was when all the information of this sort was on industry's side. The union people were in the dark. Now the large national unions have research departments headed by economists or statisticians, many of whom used to be in the employ of industrial corporations.

Does management say profits are so and so? Is the company in sound financial shape? Or is it, as it may claim, having hard sledding? The union's research department digs out data on wages, profits, and the financial status of the company. The union's publicity department will make these facts into attractive leaflets to be distributed among the employees who are union folk.

A funny incident of this type happened in negotiations between Cluett Peabody and Company and the Amalgamated Clothing Workers during a strike in 1941. The strike had begun in the

Atlanta plant and spread to the entire industry. A committee of girls from Atlanta went to the home office of the company in Troy, N. Y., to take part in negotiations.

Sitting around the table with company representatives the union's research man produced a sheet showing the salaries of each Cluett high official. Even today those would have been handsome salaries, but at that time they were high. Gasps came from the astonished Atlanta girls—think of the bosses getting such salaries while forty dollars a week was doing well for the operatives in the Cluett plants! After that an agreement was reached in short time. Cold facts about salaries had done the job.

The closer I get to the recent history of industrial unions the clearer it becomes that they are engaged in bringing a greater measure of democracy to industry and to society. With intelligent, reasonable, and honest men on both sides of the bargaining table, the duty is to find a meeting of minds between management and union. The gears of both industry and union must mesh smoothly so that the whole machinery may perform its functions.

The smooth operation of this management-union machinery means peace and production. Of the various committees set up to operate the union's affairs, the grievance or shop committee probably comes second in importance only to the bargaining committee. If this committee does its work well, it will help in preventing small troubles from growing into large ones, and may be so skillful in adjusting problems that work-stoppages will not occur because of unsettled differences.

As a final way to mediate, an arbitrator may be called in, or an arbitration committee's services asked. Many management-union contracts have provisions for arbitration. Unions have shown a much greater disposition to accept arbitration and embody it in agreements than have industries.

Local labor unions are trainers of union representatives. Men learn to think and speak on their feet, to debate with moderation, to think seriously about the matters before them. It has been thrilling through the years to see union leaders emerge and be recognized

by the members as wise, steady and courageous men to be trusted
in emergencies. Fellow members take note of such men and elect
them to responsible offices.

The same qualities that make good union leaders make good
citizens. This is evidenced in many communities through the South
(and the nation) by the union folk who take an active part in civic
and social welfare work and serve on the boards of such agencies.

As long-time observers of unions often comment they are the
seedbeds of democracy. They are also labor's colleges. In their
meetings union members discuss a great variety of subjects, as well
as those directly related to union interests. They get stimulus from
the outer world through their union papers, which give them news
from all over the United States and abroad. Committees for "the
good and welfare" are not only concerned for union members, but
for the welfare of suffering people in many nations.

The soundly democratic structure of industrial unions, composed
as they are of any race or nationality or religion that the corporation
employs, tends to break down prejudices and open the mind to
ideas of brotherliness and mutual help. The CIO lays special stress
on good relations between white and Negro people. Remarkable
achievements have been made in bringing the two races to understanding and brotherly goodwill. And in these many years in the
South I have not seen any evidence of discrimination against Jews
and Catholics in the unions.

From friends among the Catholic priesthood I understand that
a number of their seminaries are preparing students to work with
unions by courses in labor relations and economics. Many priests
have been helpful in times of strikes or when communities have
misunderstood and opposed the CIO. I recall an outstanding case
in which a priest's intervention with a company president brought
a quick end to a strike which it was feared would last for weeks.

As for sectionalism, I believe the CIO unions are doing more to
unite the South with the rest of the United States than any other
single organization. Regional prejudices have been worn at the edges
by the impact of new ideas, new personalities, union papers, state,

regional, and national gatherings, and most of all by belonging to a national or international union. Their union makes members feel a brotherhood with fellow workers in far-flung industrial plants.

The aims and motives of these industrial unions have been declared in broad social terms in each CIO national convention. They have stood four-square for things good for farmers: soil and forest conservation; rural development of electricity; the spreading of river and valley developments on the TVA pattern to the Missouri River and other localities; the social security benefits that mean so much to many millions of people; relief to people in war devastated countries. They are equally interested to see that city life is healthier and better for its people, and urge continuance of slum clearance. They are consistent in supporting federal aid to education, and also in urging larger state budgets for schools.

In fact, being men and women with children and having a concern for their fellow men, these CIO folk support what is good for people.

Among my earliest recollections is the defense by southerners of the South's errors. The South could do no wrong. As I grew older and developed a more liberal view, I shocked other southerners by pointing out our failures in democracy. It was hard to recognize there was wrong, because we were so used to it. We had assumed a complacency about this *un*-democracy which acted as a cloak to hide the truth.

The South had fought, and lost, a war to save its undemocratic system. So far as possible it kept the pattern of the old slave status. Its people looked backward for decades after the Civil War ended. Some of them still do.

Many people thought the salvation of southern society lay in keeping out democracy. Constitutions were drawn, harsh laws passed in Virginia and other states for the express purpose of denying the rights of Negroes, leaving them with no Bill of Rights—no iota of democracy. The result was that the southern states impoverished themselves—all of their citizens—by walling off from the benefits of American life a third of their people.

In recent years the wall has begun to crumble. While many forces have worked toward this end, the union movement has been at the forefront, drawing the energies of once prejudiced people into a joint endeavor that overcomes every barrier.

INDEX

Churches, Federal Council of, 179-
180, 185
and John G. Ramsay, 185-91
Methodist, 182-83
Religion and Labor Fellowship,
189, 190-91
Roman Catholic, 198
social creeds, 178-79
Southern Baptist, 180-82
and union intimidation, 183-85
Civil rights, 26, 29-30, 66, 72-73, 75-
77, 78-80, 81-84
Dublin, Ga., 124-25
Gaffney, S. C., 98-102
Giles County, Va., 117-21
Memphis, Tenn., 104-14
Tallapoosa, Ga., 121-24
Tifton, Ga., 114-17
See also Negroes
Clark, Dave, 42
Clayton, Claude, 53
Cluett Peabody & Co., 67-68, 196-
197
Cochran, J. R., 82-83
Cohen, Benjamin V., 15-16
Columbus, Ga., 20
Comer, Donald, 9
Communications Workers of Amer-
ica, 87-92, 192
Communism, 131
Congress of Industrial Organizations,
future, 193-200
leaders, 21-29
and Negroes, 164-68
Political Action Committee, 31-32
and South, 19-21, 25, 37, 147
Conn, Richard, xv
Cooper, Jerome, 62, 83
Copeland, W. A., 106
Copperhill, Tenn., 70-72
Corcoran, Tom
Cotton Textile Institute, 9-10
Cowart, John, 116-17
Cowherd, Yelverton, 58
Cox, Jimmy, 50-53
Crawford, W. H., 37, 103-4, 113,
127, 128, 132-37, 139, 141, 173,
189, 191
Crowder, Earl A., 173
Crump, Ed, 106, 112, 145, 146
Cudd, Louise, 192
Cunningham, Maj. Vincent, 191
Cuthbert, Ga., 81-84

Dallas Mill, Huntsville, Ala., 54-57
Dalrymple, Sherman, 143
Dalton, Ga., 122

Daniel, Franz, 26-27, 193-94
Darden, Governor, 158
Daugherty, Elmer, 143
Davis, Clifford, 104
Davis, Westmoreland, 6
Democratic Party, 13
Denton, Bill, 35
Denton, H. W., 38, 85
Depression, 8-9, 10, 13-14
Dewson, Mary W., 11-13, 15
Dickason, Dr. Gladys, 68, 69
Dodge, Witherspoon, 58, 99, 191
Dorsey, William, 168-70
Dowd, J. E., 39-40
Dowdle, Lee, 100
Drakes Branch, Va., 1
Dubinsky, David, 15
Dublin, Ga., 124-25
Ducktown, Tenn., 69-72
Duncan, M. E., 38
Dunn, William, 143
Dwight Manufacturing Co., 143, 144

Elder, Morton, 143
Ellijay, Ga., 96-97
Employee Representation Plan, 133
Equal Suffrage League, 4, 5
Eve, R., 115, 117

Fair Labor Practices Act, 16
Fair Labor Standards Act, 16
Farr, R. E., 142
Federal Barge Lines, 106
Federal Council of Churches, 179-
180, 185
Firestone plant, Memphis, 110-11
Fitzgerald, Harriet, 9-10
Fitzgerald, Harry, 9-10
Fitz Hugh, Alexander, 77
Flynn, Tim, 142
Ford Motor Co., 104-6
Friedman-Harry Marks Co., 65, 182

Gadsden, Ala., 142-45
Gaffney, S. C., 98-102
Gaither, Joe, 130
Garrett, Floyd, 38
Garrison, Oral, 124
Gas, Coke, and Chemical Workers,
158
General Motors Corporation, 34-38
General Shoe Co., 152
Genes, Clyde, 48-49
George Murphy, 118
Georgia News Digest, 123
Gershon, Rebecca, xv
Giles County, Va., 117-21